CLASSICAL DESTINATIONS

CLASSICAL DESTINATIONS

An armchair guide to classical music

AMADEUS
PRESS

Foreword

Most of Milos Forman's film of *Amadeus* was shot in Prague, in the studio but also in the city, much of which was exactly as it had been in the 18th century. Prague was, in fact, playing the role of Vienna in the film, although, of course, Mozart was no stranger to the Czech city. It was wonderfully inspiring to imagine him strolling (or, more likely, racing) through those streets, playing in those palaces, conducting the orchestra in that theatre — the very one in which *Don Giovanni* was first heard. People still point out the adjacent hotel where he and his librettist, Lorenzo da Ponte, communicated across the alleyway — da Ponte lobbing his latest bit of text through Mozart's open window.

Mozart was a distinguished and much appreciated visitor to Prague, but the city actually belongs, of course, to the great Bohemian composers. We now call them Czech or Slovakian, although they would not have known what we meant by these terms. The energy of the 19th century city and, above all, its central artery, the great river Vltava, is in the music of Dvořák and Smetana. But something of the 18th century city, then one of the most powerful in Europe, can be heard, too, in Mozart's symphony, nicknamed the *Prague* (his 38th) that he wrote to honour his hosts. It too bursts with the city's life and energy, but also its grandeur.

It's inconceivable that the geniuses who you will read about in this book — turbulent, passionate and avid for experience — would not have responded viscerally to their surroundings. Whatever it is that makes the architecture of Italian or German or Austrian cities so unmistakable is also to be found in the music written in those cities. They may have changed radically — very little of Berlin remains the way it was when it was a great centre of music-making — but the spirit of a city rarely changes out of all recognition. It has an identity, a personality, which is beyond alteration. Vienna, for example, has undergone an extraordinary shift in its fortunes from its 18th century zenith as the Rococo capital of the Hapsburg Empire to the culturally complex period of the Austro-Hungarian empire (during which a large amount of the city as we know it was constructed), to the neurosis of the immediate pre-First World War period when it became the crucible of the modern world, through the troubled inter-war years and the devastation that the Second World War brought, to its final and relatively becalmed manifestation in the elegant, but not especially forward-looking city of today — a place understandably hypnotised by its own past.

The unparalleled procession of great composers who lived through these transformations — Mozart, Beethoven, Schubert, Johann Strauss, Brahms, Mahler — did so very much in the present tense, responding intensely to the city in which they lived — its parks, buildings, cafés and institutions.

And so it has been for all the composers and all the cities represented in this book. Equally, one learns a great deal about cities and countries by listening to the music written there. It is two-way traffic.

It was a breathtaking experience for me to visit some of the cities with Peter Beveridge's camera crew and to stay, for instance, in the hotel in Venice where Vivaldi wrote and played some of his dazzlingly inventive concertos for every known instrumental combination, or to stand under the great Byzantine dome of San Marco and sample the acoustics which were so gloriously exploited by Monteverdi and his colleagues.

Vienna and Salzburg are eternally connected to Mozart, the latter city where he was born, almost too much so. It is impossible to walk 20 metres down the street without seeing his name or face looming up at you to persuade you to buy something — mostly the marzipan chocolates (*Mozart-kugeln*) with which his name has become inextricably identified... although a less marzipan-like composer it would be hard to imagine. How astonished he would have been — as he desperately struggled to preserve his dignity as a fairly lowly employee of the city's Prince-Archbishop — if he had been given a glimpse of his own mass-marketing. But Mozart was a practical fellow, much involved with the problems of making a living, and it's to be hoped that given such a glimpse he might have managed at least to arrange, for the benefit of his offspring, a healthy percentage of the millions made in his name

An experience of an altogether different nature is to be found just outside of the Finnish capital of Helsinki, in 'Ainola', the house Jean Sibelius and his wife Aino created as a place where he could compose. It's an unpretentious sort of a *dacha* in the countryside only a few miles from the city, but deep in the heart of nature.

The moment one crosses the homely hearth one becomes aware of a quite uncommon stillness. Here the great man completed his monumental symphonic cycle and wrote the Violin Concerto and those forbidding masterpieces *En Saga* and *Tapiola*, as well as a lot of genial and sometimes stirring occasional music. He composed not at the piano, but in his head and absolute silence was his requirement to the extent that he refused to allow plumbing to be installed in the house — its noise would have disturbed his concentration. Even today, the only sound that can be heard, in fact — apart from the odd distant motorcar or aeroplane — is the sound of the wind sighing in the trees that surround the house, the sound that echoes through so much of his music. Here, the place that has influenced the composer is not a city, but somewhere of his own making, the "symphony of wood," as he called it. Here too, repose the mortal remains of the composer and his wife. It's a beautiful and a serene setting, the tomb itself is a thing of austere simplicity, linear and abstract — a monument to the distilled power the composer struggled, to such profound effect, to achieve in his work.

It's impossible not to hear Sibelius's music differently after a visit to 'Ainola' and the same, we hope, is true of all our classical destinations.

SIMON CALLOW

Simon Callow with Sibelius's piano at the Finnish composer's home 'Ainola', near Helsinki.

Destinations

Schubert Brahms Haydn

Salzburg

…Any place that had been
the birthplace of a Mozart would
be perfectly entitled to boast about it
hundreds of years later. It helps that Salzburg
is so staggeringly beautiful, of course. In
death, Mozart is more consistently
present in his hometown than he
ever was during his short life…

Simon Callow

$\mathcal{M}$ention Salzburg to anyone who has been there and they get a far away look in their eyes, smile softly and murmur, "Ah... Salzburg", and with good reason. The geography of Salzburg and its nearly perfectly preserved baroque 'Old Town' conspire to make it a historical and cultural destination that dreams are made of.

Established on the banks of the River Salzach, Salzburg was originally a Celtic settlement and then a Roman centre of trade. In 696 AD St Rupert founded a monastery here which became an archbishopric with authority over a great part of southern Germany. In the 13th century, the archbishops were granted the title of Princes of the Holy Roman Empire, beginning the rule of the Prince-Archbishops of Salzburg which continued until the unification of Austria in 1815. Their economic power was based largely on salt and silver mined from the mountains around the town. Salzburg literally means 'Castle of Salt'.

The city is the birthplace of the composer considered by many to be the greatest ever — Mozart. It was in a third floor apartment at Getreidegasse 9, that Mozart was born on 27 January 1756. It became known as the Hagenauer House after the surname of the owner from whom the Mozart family rented the apartment.

Mozart was christened Joannes Chrysostomus Wolfgangus Theophilus Mozart. So perhaps it's not surprising he preferred the name 'Amadeo' — and not Amadeus — which he later coined himself. Wolfgang's father, Leopold, was a violin teacher and instrumentalist in the court of the Prince-Archbishop. He was an accomplished composer of concertos, symphonies, chamber music, songs, cantatas and masses, as well as an early book of violin technique.

Leopold actually wrote much more than his more famous son. He recognised the precocious nature of his son's talent at a very early age — Wolfgang was playing harpsichord from the age of three, and his earliest composition was written when he was five. Wolfgang's older sister, Nannerl, was also extremely talented, and Leopold took the two of them on concert tours through Europe. Mozart was just six.

Through Leopold's connections, they played for everyone from fellow musicians through to the crowned heads of England, France and Austria. All were impressed. So much so that, after one concert, the Emperor and Empress of Austria encouraged young Wolfgang to write an opera. He duly obliged with an opera in Italian, *La Finta Semplice*, written in 1769 when he was aged 12.

PREVIOUS PAGES: The Festung Hohensalzburg over looks the city of Salzburg and can be reached by foot or a funicular railway. The fortress dates back to 1077 and is built on the site of a Roman castrum.

The interior of Stiftskirche St Peter (St Peter's Cathedral). The church dates back to the mid-12th century, but was extensively redesigned in the 18th century and contains many Baroque-style frescoes and ornamentation. INSET: The entrance to the cathedral.

OPPOSITE: The name Salzburg literally means 'Castle of Salt' and was derived from the rock salt mined from the surrounding mountains. The location was first settled in Celtic times and later became a Roman administrative centre.

ABOVE LEFT: Salzburg is Mozart's city; his presence is everywhere… including this lifesize cut-out selling, of all things, chocolates bearing his profile.

WOLFGANG AMADEUS MOZART AT A GLANCE

Among classical music's most gifted composers, Wolfgang Amadeus Mozart was born in Salzburg on 27 January 1756. The son of a court musician, he began showing an interest in music when aged just three and by five he was already composing short pieces. His father, Leopold, saw financial potential in the boy's burgeoning talent and embarked on a concert tour through Europe's royal courts. In Vienna Wolfgang, not yet six, and his older sister Maria Anna (known as 'Nannerl' and also a child prodigy) performed for the Empress Maria Theresa and her daughter, Marie Antoinette. Such was the success of this tour that another followed – lasting three-and-a-half years – which included a visit to London. The family returned to Salzburg in late 1766 by which time Mozart had already composed his first symphony. His first opera, *La Finta Semplice*, was written in 1768, commissioned following a recommendation by Emperor Joseph II.

In 1769 Wolfgang and Leopold commenced another tour, this time to Italy where the boy, still not yet 14, was received in Rome by Pope Clement XIV. Back in Salzburg, Mozart's output was prodigious and included symphonies, operas, Masses, violin concertos, serenades and divertimenti. In 1777 he visited Paris, this time with his mother who became ill and died during the trip. In 1779 Mozart was appointed court organist at Salzburg and concentrated on producing music for the church as well as more symphonies and divertimenti. However, he was increasingly unhappy in his position

and an acrimonious parting with the Archbishop led to Mozart moving to Vienna to become a freelance musician... seemingly one of the first to try to make a living without either a position or patronage.

In 1718 he married Constanze Weber who bore him six children, although only two survived. While it appears the couple struggled financially, some of his most beautiful and celebrated music comes from this period, including six string quartets dedicated to Haydn. Also written at this time was his best known opera, *The Marriage of Figaro*, first performed in Vienna on 1 May 1786. A huge success, Mozart followed it with another, *Don Giovanni*, which premiered in Prague in October 1787.

Unfortunately, his financial circumstances continued to worsen and, forced to find paid work, Mozart was appointed court-composer to the Emperor. He turned down a more lucrative position in Berlin and faced even more dire financial circumstances when Constanze became ill and medical bills needed to be paid.

Another of Mozart's great operas, *Così fan tutte*, had its debut in Vienna in early 1790, but failed to help him financially. Burdened by anxiety, overwork and malnourishment, Mozart's health began to fail, but in his final year he still managed to produce two quintets (in D major and E flat), a piano concerto (in B flat) and The Magic Flute. Ironically, Mozart's final work was a Requiem Mass, left unfinished when he died, aged 35, on 5 December 1791.

The apartment on Getreidegasse was the Mozart family home between 1747 and 1773, and is now the Mozart's Geburtshaus museum. On display are some remarkable items including Mozart's clavichord, his piano and the violin he played as a child, as well as an assortment of original manuscripts, memorabilia and family portraits.

The rear of Hagenauer House looks over the town market and even today is a focal point. Across the square, Tomaselli's has been serving coffee, in the tradition for which Salzburg is famous, since the early 1700s. The original Italian owner, Señor Tomaselli, was an accomplished tenor. Mozart also enjoyed the ambience at Tomaselli's, although it's said he once wrote a letter of complaint about the quality of the coffee.

The Mirabell Palace was first built in 1606 by Prince-Archbishop Wolf Dietrich who was largely responsible for the present shape of the old town. The palace was originally named Altenau after his mistress, Salome von Alt, who had 15 children to the aptly named Wolf. Sadly for Salome, Wolf got the sack in 1612 and she had to follow. The new Archbishop changed the name to Mirabell. The building was destroyed by fire in 1818 so the current palace is a reconstruction.

Mozart's Geburtshaus. This is where the composer was born on 27 January 1756 and where he composed his earliest works. Now a museum, it contains many items from Mozart's childhood, including instruments.

High above the Old Town is the imposing castle known as Festung Hohensalzburg or the High Salzburg Fortress. It was built — on the site of a Roman fort — by Archbishop Gebhard I in 1077 and for the next 700 years was continuously being extended so it's actually become a small, self-contained town. Today it's the largest, fully preserved fortress in Europe.

Over the centuries the fortress has also been used as a prison and as a military base, but now it houses a museum, restaurants and a gift shop. Regular evening concerts are held here, but the really breathtaking aspect of the place is the view. The glory of Salzburg is spread out below and, on the other three sides, is the majesty of the Austrian Alps.

In the 16th and 17th centuries, the Prince-Archbishops imported a lot of architectural styles from the Imperial capital of Rome to build their palaces and cathedrals. So much so that Salzburg is often referred to as the 'Rome of the north'. St Peter's Abbey and Salzburg Cathedral are classic examples. The cemetery at St Peter's is the oldest in Austria still in use.

A short walk away is the Mozarteum University, founded in 1841, which is internationally renowned and offers over 30 courses in music, performing and the fine arts. Many graduates of the university have achieved international renown, including the legendary German conductor, Herbert von Karajan.

As fashionable as the Archbishops were, they didn't have a monopoly on style. The Hotel Goldener Hirsch — in the heart of the Old Town — was originally a 15th century inn. It's now magnificently preserved for 21st century guests, with a style all its own. Many speakers, composers,

maestros and guest artists stay here for the annual Salzburg Festival. First held in 1920, the festival includes opera, drama and concerts presented at venues around the city over a period of five to six weeks every July and August. An integral part of the festival is a series of Mozart concerts, but an event dedicated to the composer — Mozart Week — is held every January to celebrate his birthday.

Not long after the movie *The Sound of Music* was released in 1965, tourists starting visiting Salzburg and calling it 'the city of *The Sound of Music*'. There is still a '*Sound of Music*' Dinner Show in the historic Sternbrau restaurant. The show includes most musical highlights from the movie and opens with a recorded interview with the real Maria von Trapp (the family eventually settled in Vermont in the USA).

The palace and gardens at Schloss Hellbrunn, just south of Salzburg, were built by Archbishop Marcus Sitticus between 1613 and 1615 and are indicative of the opulence of the Prince-Archbishops. Built in the style of an Italian villa, the castle and its grounds were completed in a remarkably short time even by modern standards. Hellbrunn is a unique fusion of the arts — sculpture, frescoes, paintings by Italian masters and a collection of elaborate trick fountains.

ABOVE: A view over Salzburg from the Festung Hohensalzburg.

OPPOSITE: The main stairwell in the Schloss Mirabell. The palace originates from the early 17th century and was extensively redesigned from 1721 to 1727, but was virtually destroyed by fire in 1818. Today's building is a reconstruction of the redesigned palace.

FOLLOWING PAGES: The Schloss Mirabell is surrounded by extensive formal gardens containing many fountains and statues. Today the palace houses the mayor's office.

The Mirabell Palace was first built in 1606 by

Prince-Archbishop Wolf Dietrich who was largely

responsible for the present shape of the old town.

WEBSITE – www.salzburg.info

COMPOSERS – Wolfgang Amadeus Mozart, Johann Michael Haydn.

POPULATION – 147,000.

CLIMATE

WINTER – cold with average temperatures in the region of -2 degrees Celsius, snowfall is common.

SPRING – daytime temperatures vary from around 8 to 20 degrees Celsius, warm winds can raise temperatures.

SUMMER – daytime temperatures can rise to around 28 to 30 degrees Celsius, but thunderstorms and rainy periods are frequent. June typically experiences up to 19 to 20 rainy days.

AUTUMN – daytime temperatures range from 18 to 25 degrees Celsius.

BEST TIME OF THE YEAR TO VISIT – Any time of the year.

TOP FIVE TOURIST ATTRACTIONS

FESTUNG HOHENSALZBURG – imposing fortress dating back to the 11th century.

MOZART'S BIRTHPLACE AND RESIDENCE – two different buildings. The composer's birthplace is at Getreidegasse 9 and, after returning from Vienna in 1773, he lived at Makartplatz 8.

MUSEUM OF NATURAL HISTORY (Haus der Natur) – includes a 40-tank aquarium and a reptile house, Museumsplatz 5.

SCHLOSS HELLBRUNN – Archbishop's palace, just south of Salzburg, surrounded by extensive gardens.

RESIDENZ – 16th century bishop's palace containing 15 lavishly appointed state rooms.

TOP TWO COFFEE HOUSES

Café Tomaselli (over 300 years old), Alter Markt 9.

Café Fürst.

MUST SEE SHOPPING LOCATIONS

GETREIDEGASSE – the main thoroughfare of Old Salzburg and a shopper's paradise.

ALTER MARKT – the old market, including an original pharmacy dating back to 1591

LINZERGASSE – shops specialising in clothing, shoes and consumer goods.

COMPOSERS MUSEUMS/HOMES

MOZART'S GEBURTSHAUS (Mozart's birthplace), Getreidegasse 9.

MOZART WOHNHAUS (Mozart's residence for seven years from 1773), MAKARTPLATZ 8. Houses original manuscripts and period furniture.

JOHANN MICHAEL HAYDN GEDENKSTÄTTE at the Stiftskirche St Peter, memorial to Joseph Haydn's younger brother who was the organist at this 12th century church from 1777.

GARDENS/PARKS MUST SEE

Mirabell Gardens – formal gardens surrounding the Schloss Mirabell and famous for its statues.

Hellbrunn Park – a fantastic collection of trick fountains, water spouts and grottoes.

ANNUAL MUSICAL EVENTS

January – Mozart Week (Mozart Woche), www.mozarteum.at

March/April – Easter Festival, www.osterfestspiele-salzburg.at

May – Salzburg Whitsun Baroque Music Festival, www.salzburgfestival.at

July/August – Salzburg Festival, an annual tribute to Mozart, www.salzburgfestival.at

October/November – Salzburger Jazzherbst (Autumn Jazz Festival), www.panoramatours.com

October – Culture Days (last two weeks of the month).

INFORMATION AND TICKETS

Salzburg Information, Auerspergstrasse 6, Salzburg 5020, telephone +43 (0662) 889 870, email tourist@salzurg.info or visit www.salzburg.info

In 1769 — aged 13 — Mozart was appointed as the unsalaried *Konzertmeister*, the concertmaster, of the Salzburg Court Orchestra. At the end of the year, father and son set out on an extended journey to Italy, visiting Verona, Milan, Florence, Rome and Naples. Wolfgang met with success at every stage. His opera, *Mitridate, Rè di Ponto* was first staged in Milan and, still only 14, he conducted the performance himself.

In December 1771, the Prince-Archbishop — who was also the Mozarts' employer — died. Despite being contracted to the court, Leopold and Wolfgang had been allowed to travel wherever and whenever they wanted. The new Archbishop, Hieronymus, was less accommodating. At first everything was fine, but while young Wolfgang may have been brilliant musically, it seems he was badly lacking in tact and soon had offended the Archbishop. However, to be fair to Wolfgang,

BELOW: The Schloss Leopoldskroner and its lake, just south of Salzburg, was one of the locations for the Sound Of Music. *Cue the swan...*

Hieronymus was strict and narrow-minded particularly in regard to cultural matters.

In 1773, the Mozarts moved to the Tanzmeisterhaus — the dance master's house. Severely damaged by bombing in 1944, it has been painstakingly and beautifully restored, and today is a museum.

It soon became apparent to Wolfgang that he would never have a decent job in Salzburg so, over the next four years, he tried desperately to find an appointment somewhere else in Europe.

"How I detest Salzburg," he wrote, "Salzburg is no place for my talent...".

ABOVE AND RIGHT: The Renaissance prince-archbishop Wolf Dietrich von Raitenau wanted to turn Salzburg into the 'Rome of the North' and employed Italian architects and designers on many building projects (including the cathedral).

OPPOSITE TOP: The Mozart Wohnhaus is where the composer lived from 1773 to 1780 and today contains original manuscripts, memorabilia and period furniture.

OPPOSITE BELOW: The Café Tomaselli was patronised by Mozart.

In 1778, after a brief illness, Wolfgang's mother tragically died while accompanying him on a trip to Paris where he had conducted the 'Paris Symphony' (*Symphony no. 31 in D major*). Back in Salzburg, the Archbishop still appeared intent on keeping Wolfgang on a short leash. Finally in June 1781, after numerous conflicts with Hieronymus — and apparently against his father's desires — he resigned from the Salzburg court and headed to Vienna.

As a postscript to the Tanzmeisterhaus, Nannerl continued living there with her father until she married in 1784 and moved to nearby St Gilgen. Leopold was left alone and died in 1787.

In such a glorious setting it's no wonder that Leopold and Anna Maria Mozart should name their only son after their beloved St Wolfgang.

IN DEN SOMMERMONATEN
DER JAHRE 1893-1896
WOHNTE IN DIESEM HAUSE
GUSTAV MAHLER
1860   1911
HIER ENTSTANDEN DIE
II. UND III. SYMPHONIE

On their journeys between Salzburg and Vienna, the Mozarts travelled through some of the most picturesque country in Europe. The village of St Gilgen, on the Wolfgangsee (lake) is the birthplace of Mozart's mother, Anna Maria Pertl, and her family came from the region including the nearby village of St Wolfgang. In such a glorious setting it's little wonder that Leopold and Anna Maria Mozart should name their only son after the lake and village. Mozart, however, isn't the only classical composer to have connections in this part of the world.

Nearby Steinbach, on the lake called Attersee, was a welcome retreat for Gustav Mahler in the 1890s. At the time, he was living in Hamburg, but found the bustle of the city and the hectic theatre season wasn't conducive to the creative process. The Gasthof zum Höllengebirge in Steinbach — a still-operating inn — solved his problem. Mahler also built

PREVIOUS PAGES: *The beautiful village of St Wolfgang is typical of many in the spectacular Salzkammergut region of Austria. Mozart's mother was born in a nearby village, St Gilgen, and named her only son after St Wolfgang and its lake (the Wolfgangsee)*

OPPOSITE TOP, THIS PAGE TOP AND BELOW: *In the 1890s Gustav Mahler built a composer's hut at Steinbach on the Attersee.*

OPPOSITE BELOW: *Mozart often travelled through Linz, but he stayed here for a number of weeks in 1783 as a guest of Count von Thun and later wrote the 'Linz Symphony' (No.36 in C major).*

a small composer's cottage on the edge of the lake where much of his music was written. With so much time spent here, he became known as the 'vacation composer'.

Linz, on the River Danube, is one of the largest cities in Austria, and Mozart often broke his journey here. In 1783 he and his wife, Constanze Weber (whom he had married a year earlier), visited Linz on their way back to Vienna from Salzburg. They'd only planned to spend a night, but ended up staying three weeks as guests of a Count von Thun. During this time, Mozart composed his *Symphony No. 36 in C major*. Known as the 'Linz Symphony', it was first performed at the Linz Theatre on 4 November 1783, only a few days after it was finished.

Not to be outdone by Salzburg, Linz has its Bruckner festival — honouring the composer Anton Bruckner — which runs for three weeks from mid-September. It starts with the 'Classical Cloud of Sound' — over 200,000 watts of classical music power broadcast throughout Danube Park. The festival brings together many famous conductors, orchestras and soloists for public performances. Bruckner was, for a time, the organist at the Old Cathedral in Linz, and the Brucknerhaus, built in the early 1970s, is among Europe's most famous modern concert halls.

On the way to Linz from Vienna is the town of Melk with

The beautiful village of Dürnstein in the Wachau region of Austria is situated on the River Danube and includes a Baroque monastery with a distinctive blue-and-white steeple.

its 900 year-old abbey. In 1767, the Mozart family, including Wolfgang then aged 11, interrupted their journey to tour the abbey. Further down the Danube is the stunning little village of Dürnstein. Apart from a baroque monastery, Dürnstein's other claim to fame is the legend of Richard the Lionheart and his minstrel, Blondel, who heralded his imprisoned master as a means of recognition. From Dürnstein, it's only a short drive to the grand old city of Vienna.

Vienna

...Beethoven must have felt
so unjustifiably conspired against
by Fate: going deaf, and being so eternally
unhappy in love. Writing music was his only
recourse, and he sometimes used it like a fist,
hammering out those long symphonic finales,
or being 'Fate knocking on the door',
as he described the beginning
of his Fifth Symphony...

SIMON CALLOW

V ienna was originally a Roman outpost that was almost completely levelled by the barbarians, but then resurrected by Charlemagne in the late 8th or early 9th century. He established a territory called Ostmark — Austria — and in 976 the Babenberg dukes were installed as rulers by the Holy Roman Emperor Otto II in 976. They ruled Austria for nearly 300 years, during which time Vienna grew in stature as a major trading centre.

As the Babenberg dynasty ended in the mid-13th century, a new order came to prominence in Austria. The Hapsburgs stayed in power for over 600 years, at times presiding over dominions so widespread that it was said to be an empire on which the sun never set.

Although the Hapsburgs weren't totally innocent, what set them apart from most of the other ruling families in Europe at the time was that, rather than using the sword to gain their lands, they employed 'weapons' such as marriage and diplomacy. This helps explain the wealth and depth of art, music and architecture that has become Vienna's heritage into the 21st century.

In 1857, Franz Josef I, the last Hapsburg emperor, ordered that the wall around the city be torn down. It was replaced by a broad boulevard called the Ringstrasse on which were built many new public buildings in various architectural styles. 'The Ring' is four kilometres long and circles the city centre. Taking a tram around the Ring is the best way to see many of the remarkable buildings, including the Fine Art Museum which houses one of the world's richest and most important art collections. It was amassed by the Hapsburgs, and includes works by Rubens, Rembrandt, Vermeer, Dürer, Raphael, Titian and Velázquez, as well as the largest collection of Brueghel's paintings in the world. There's also a huge collection of ancient Egyptian, Greek and Roman artefacts as well as sculpture and decorative art.

The Vienna State Opera House was completed in 1869. Built in the style of the Italian Renaissance, on the loggia at the front is a cycle

FRANZ SCHUBERT AT A GLANCE

Of all the classical composers with a connection to Vienna, Franz Peter Schubert undoubtedly has the closest links, having been born in the city, and subsequently living there his entire life. He was born on 31 January 1797, in Viennese suburb of Lichtenthal, one of only three Schubert children – out of 11 – to survive infancy.

Franz's musical talent was evident early on and his formal musical education commenced when he was ten. The following year, in 1808, he was accepted as a choirboy at the court chapel in Vienna which also guaranteed entry into the exclusive Stadtkonvikt boarding school. Here he quickly progressed to lead violin in the school orchestra, and he was taught composition by Antonio Salieri who had also been tutor to Beethoven (and a rival to Mozart).

Schubert began composing while still at school and both his talent for melodic fluency and ability to write for the voice were immediately apparent. Nevertheless, he followed his father's wishes and trained to become a teacher. In 1814 he became an assistant teacher, but continued to compose prolifically. During the next year alone he wrote two symphonies, three sonatas, two Masses, six operas and nearly 150 songs including *Erlkönig*, a setting from Goethe's *Faust* which became his most celebrated work.

In mid-1818 Schubert took up the position as music teacher to the court of Esterházy and moved to Hungary,

but he quickly missed Vienna and returned to Austria by the end of the year. The next summer, while holidaying in rural Steyr, Schubert wrote the popular *Trout Quintet* and he was in constant demand to play at social evenings and dances.

In 1822 Schubert contracted syphilis which required hospitalisation. He had begun writing his *Symphony No.8 in B minor* which was never finished and hence became known as the 'Unfinished Symphony'. While in hospital he wrote the song cycle *Die Schöne Müllerin* and continued to compose while recuperating in first Linz and then Steyr. His health was now continually poor, but his musical talent remained undiminished and, in the last five years of his life, Schubert produced such masterpieces as his piano sonatas in A minor and D major, *Die Allmacht* (considered one of his most magnificent songs), the 24-song cycle *Die Winterreise* and the immense *Symphony No.9 in C major* (later called 'The Great').

In March 1827 Schubert visited the dying Beethoven and was subsequently a torch-bearer at his funeral. After catching typhoid, a not uncommon occurrence given the poor hygiene standards of the day, Franz Schubert himself died on 19 November 1828, aged just 31. While his was clearly a life cut short, his prodigious talent and output ensured Schubert left behind a magnificent musical legacy, and the right to be considered an equal of Haydn, Mozart and Beethoven.

showing, among other operas, scenes from Mozart's *The Magic Flute*. The Opera House is famous for many reasons — first-class opera performances, the Vienna Philharmonic Orchestra and the people who have performed here. Gustav Mahler was conductor at the Opera House for ten years from 1897 to 1907.

Franz Schubert was born in Liechtental in Vienna in 1797. Like so many of the great composers, he had an abnormal ability to learn quickly at an early age. Schubert didn't have a formal education, but because of his talent, he was accepted as a chorister at the Court Chapel at the age of 11. Here he studied composition under Antonio Salieri (who also taught Beethoven) and, by the time he left in 1813, he had already completed his first symphony.

Schubert's family were devout Catholics and their local church is now called the Schubertkirche. Although he composed a lot of religious music, Schubert was renowned for enjoying a good party. He seemed to thrive on setting poetry to music and wrote nearly 600 songs as well as nine symphonies, ten operas, string quartets, piano sonatas and numerous choral pieces. Schubert venerated Beethoven and considered him to be a "guiding star". He held a torch at Beethoven's funeral which was held in Vienna in 1827.

On 19 November 1828, Schubert himself died, aged 31, of typhoid fever. Unfortunately, like so many before him, Franz Schubert's work was not widely recognised until after his death. During his lifetime he gave only one public concert and died penniless

Born in Hamburg in 1833, Johannes Brahms moved to Vienna after his friend, fellow German composer Robert Schumann, died in 1856.

Brahms has been described as "a rock of classicism in the rushing stream of new styles" and he didn't start composing until he was about

LEFT: Gustav Mahler (whose bust is seen here) was the conductor at the Vienna State Opera from 1897 to 1907.

BELOW: Vienna's State Opera House was designed in the Italian Renaissance style.

ABOVE LEFT: Brahms once commented that he lived in Vienna because he could only work in a village… the Austrian capital still retains a friendly 'small town' atmosphere. ABOVE RIGHT: The Heiligenstadt House where, in 1802, Beethoven wrote what has since become known as 'the Heiligenstadt Testament' in which he informed his brothers of his deafness. OPPOSITE: Vienna's Gothic Stephansdom (cathedral) features an elaborately tiled roof. The two Romanesque towers are known as the Heidenturme or the 'Pagan Towers'.

20, although again he showed musical talent while still young. Slow and painstaking, he was 43 before he completed his first symphony which took 14 years to finish. In 1853 he was given a letter of introduction to Robert Schumann and his wife Clara. They became close friends and, after Schumann was institutionalised following a failed suicide attempt, Clara became the great love of his life. It seems, though, that the two were only ever very close friends even after Schumann died.

During Brahms' time in Vienna he became a master of every form of composition — except opera which he never attempted. It was in Vienna that he first experienced real success with his *German Requiem* and *Variations on a theme of Haydn*. Not long after this — and because of the success of his *Symphony No. 1 in C minor* — he was hailed as the true successor to Beethoven. Indeed, this symphony was proclaimed at the time as 'Beethoven's Tenth'.

Brahms was devoted to the traditional compositional forms, and once said, "If we cannot compose as beautifully as Mozart and Haydn, let us at least try to compose as purely".

Critical of what he saw as the "progressive" musical styles of contemporaries Franz Liszt, Anton Bruckner and Richard Wagner, Brahms frequently felt the pressure of following the classical masters and this self-imposed discipline was one reason he struggled with many of his compositions. He died in Vienna in April 1897.

The Hapsburg palace of Schloss Schönbrunn, just outside Vienna, is a classic example of the wealth, opulence and power of the family which ruled Austria and its empire for over 600 years. In 1612, Emperor Matthias discovered what he called "the fair spring" — *die schönner brunnen* — which gave the estate its name. The following year a hunting lodge was built in the gardens and the zoo on the site was opened in 1752, making it the oldest in the world. A palace — intended to rival Versailles in its scope and grandeur — was commenced in the late 17th century during the reign of Leopold I. However, it wasn't until his grand-daughter, Maria Theresa, came to the throne that the golden years of Schönbrunn began.

In the palace's Hall of Mirrors Mozart gave his first concert for Maria Theresa and her husband Franz Stephan, in 1762 at the age of six. Legend has it that at the end of the concert young Wolfgang leapt on to Maria Theresa's lap and kissed her. During the same visit Mozart was playing with the young princesses and slipped on the polished wooden floor. Bursting into tears, he was picked up and comforted by the seven-year-old Princess Marie Antoinette. Mozart is said to have kissed her and proposed marriage. The young princess probably should have accepted because, of course, she eventually became the wife of Louis XVI of France. Ironically, after the revolution which saw Marie Antoinette beheaded, Napoleon used Schloss Schönbrunn as his command centre during his invasion of Austria in 1809.

After Mozart moved to Vienna in 1781, he and Constanze were married the next year. The couple lived in a number of places, but

The magnificent Schloss Schönbrunn is a huge palace which includes the Hall of Mirrors where Mozart, aged just six, played for the Empress Maria Theresa. The palace is surrounded by a 185-hectare park which includes the world's oldest zoo.

THIS PAGE AND PREVIOUS
PAGES: The palace at Schönbrunn was
designed by the architect Nikolaus
Pacassi who was commissioned by
Maria Theresa... she wanted a building
to rival Versailles. Above is a detail from
the room where Mozart performed and
below is a portrait of the Empress Maria
Theresa.

WEBSITE: www.vienna.info

COMPOSERS: Franz Schubert, Arnold Schönberg, Johann Strauss I, Johann Strauss II were all born in Vienna. Ludwig van Beethoven, Anton Bruckner, Johannes Brahms, Gaetano Donizetti, Joseph Haydn, Christoph von Gluck, Franz Liszt, Gustav Mahler, Antonio Salieri and Wolfgang Amadeus Mozart all lived here at some stage.

POPULATION: 1.6 million.

CLIMATE

WINTER — daily temperatures typically range from -2 to 9 degrees Celsius, winds can lower temperatures considerably.

SPRING — daily temperatures range from 2 to 20 degrees Celsius.

SUMMER — daily temperatures range from 13 to 35 degrees Celsius, mostly hot and dry.

AUTUMN — daily temperatures range from 6 to 25 degrees Celsius.

BEST TIME OF THE YEAR TO VISIT: March to May, and August to October.

TOP FIVE TOURIST ATTRACTIONS

UPPER BELVEDERE PALACE — the Austrian Gallery which houses masterpieces by Klimt, Schiele and Kokoschka.

HOFBURG — the royal palace, includes many museums and the Burgkapelle where the Vienna Boys Choir sing mass (except during July and August).

MUSEUMSQUARTIER — includes the Leopold Museum, the MUMOK (the modern arts museum) and the Kunsthalle (housing, among other things, a children's museum and a tobacco museum).

SCHLOSS SCHÖNBRUNN — a palace built to rival Versailles in its grandeur.

THE RINGSTRASSE and its historic buildings (take a tram) — the Opera House, Museum

of Fine Arts, Museum of Applied Arts, the Parliament building, the Burgtheater (the National Theatre), the Rathaus (City Hall) and the Schönborn Palais.

TOP TWO COFFEE HOUSES

Café Central, Herrengasse 14.

Café Hawelka, Dorotheergasse 6.

MUST SEE SHOPPING LOCATIONS

Kärntner Strasse, Graben and Kohlmarkt.

Mariahilfer Strasse/Neubaugasse.

Freihaus-Quarter with its famous Schleifmühlgasse.

COMPOSERS MUSEUMS/HOMES

FIGAROHAUS (Mozart's home where he composed The Marriage of Figaro), Domgasse 5, www.mozarthausvienna.at

HAYDN MEMORIAL, Haydngasse 19

HOUSE OF THE EROICA (Beethoven's home), Döblinger Hauptstrasse 92

ARNOLD SCHÖNBERG CENTRE, Zaunergasse 1-3, www.schoenber.at

FRANZ SCHUBERT'S BIRTHPLACE, Nussdorfer Strasse 54

THE DANUBE WALTZ HOUSE (Johann Strauss' home), Praterstrasse 54

GARDENS/PARKS MUST SEE

Schloss Schönbrunn — magnificent parklands surrounding Empress Maria Theresa's palace,

and including the world's oldest zoo.

Wiener Prater — formerly imperial hunting grounds, today famous for its giant Ferris Wheel.

Danube Island — Vienna's 'recreation paradise' of beaches, cycle ways and playgrounds

Stadtpark (City Park) — contains busts of composers including Johann Strauss

Volksgarten (Common Gardens) — also visit the nearby Parlament designed by Theophil Hansen.

ANNUAL MUSICAL EVENTS

March to April/May — Vienna Spring Festival, an extensive program of classical concerts, www.konzerthaus.at

May to June — Vienna Festival (Wiener Festwochen), international performers in opera, music and dance; www.festwochen.at

June to July — Jazz Festival Vienna (Jazz Fest Wien), www.viennajazz.org

July to August — KlangBogen (Summer Music), opera, chamber music and orchestral works, www.klangbogen.at

Easter — OsterKlang (Easter Music), www.klangbogen.at

INFORMATION

Austrian Tourist Information Centre (Österreich Werbung), Margaretenstrasse 1, Vienna 1040, telephone +43 (01) 587 2000, or visit www.austria-tourism.at

their favourite was what is now called Figarohaus — The Figaro House — because this is where Mozart composed his opera *Le Nozze di Figaro* — *The Marriage of Figaro*. In fact, some of his greatest compositions were created in this house, including a number of piano concertos and string quartets. At one of Mozart's concerts during this period, it's said that Joseph Haydn was sitting next to Leopold Mozart and observed, "We shall not see such another great genius for a hundred years".

The Figaro House was a very large apartment for the time and a sign of success and wealth — and Mozart had always been very concerned about appearances. It's just a short walk to the magnificent Stephansdom (St Stephen's Cathedral), commenced in the mid-12th century and completed around 200 years later. Mozart and Constanze were married here — as was Strauss — and Mozart's funeral was held here. Haydn and Schubert sang here as choirboys. In 1791 Mozart was appointed assistant to the cathedral's *Kapellmeister*. It was an unpaid position, but if he had lived another couple of years, there is little doubt he would have been promoted.

Mozart experienced mixed success in Vienna. At times he was the darling of the Royal Court, but at other times, his work wasn't so well received and he was often left penniless and in debt. He was probably better received in Prague than in his beloved Vienna. When *Figaro* opened in Vienna, it only played nine times, but in Prague it received tumultuous acclaim and

The monument to Mozart in St Marx Cemetery where it's thought the composer was buried. As Mozart died a pauper he was buried in a mass grave and the exact whereabouts of his body isn't known.

W. A. MOZART

1756-1791

led to the commissioning of *Don Giovanni* which was also premiered in the city as was *Symphony No. 38 in D major* otherwise known as the 'Prague Symphony'.

Mozart's final work was the *Requiem* and was commissioned anonymously, although it's been suggested that he was writing it for himself. He was still working on it when he died of rheumatic fever in the early hours of 5 December 1791, aged 35. Remarkably, Wolfgang Amadeus Mozart died a pauper and, consequently, was buried in a common mass grave, the exact location of which still remains unknown.

The historic Palais of the Archduke Charles in central Vienna is an amazing place today, called the 'House of Music'. It's a modern, interactive museum dedicated to sound and music. The first floor is dedicated to the Vienna Philharmonic Orchestra and visitors are 'greeted' by a life-like effigy of the founder — the composer and conductor, Otto Nicolai. The second floor is an incredible mix of sound in all its forms and the latest technology in a hands-on environment, taking interactivity to a new level. The third floor is devoted to every great composer who lived and worked in Vienna from Haydn to Mahler and beyond to the second Viennese School of composers in the 20th century.

The Theater-an-der-Wien has been the site of many a significant premiere. Among them Johann Strauss' opera *Die Fledermaus* and numerous premieres by the composer who rivals Mozart for the title of the greatest who ever lived — Ludwig van Beethoven.

TOP: The Beethoven exhibition and interactive 'experience' in Vienna's House of Music.

ABOVE: A selection of Beethoven memorabilia and documents in Eroica House

Beethoven was born in Bonn in 1770 and was first published musically at the age of 12. When 17 he came to Vienna to study under Mozart who was impressed with his improvisational skills on the piano. However, shortly after arriving, Beethoven had to return to Bonn after he heard his mother was seriously ill. He returned to Vienna in 1792 where he studied under Haydn (Mozart having died the previous year). A restless character, he is believed to have lived in over 60 different places in the city, including rooms in the Theater-an-der-Wien. A favourite was known as the Pasqualati House after its owner. Here Beethoven worked on several of his most important compositions, including the fourth, fifth, seventh and eighth symphonies and his only opera, *Fidelio*.

Beethoven moved in and out of the Pasqualati House usually after quarrels with the owner over the composer's habit of playing the piano with gusto well into the early hours of the morning.

Completed in 1804 Beethoven's epic *Symphony No. 3 in E flat major* — the *'Eroica'* — is considered an important milestone in classical music history. With its new 'heroic' style and emotional depth, Beethoven began to break free of the more traditional forms of Haydn and Mozart. Up until this point music had been viewed primarily as entertainment and nobody had considered that, like literature, a work could reveal the composer's view of the world. With *Eroica*, Beethoven is credited with changing this attitude and, in so doing, ushered in the 'the romantic era' in classical music. Incidentally, it was originally to be called the 'Bonaparte Symphony' in honour of Napoleon's deposing of the French monarchy. However, when Napoleon then declared himself Emperor of France,

ABOVE: Classical Destinations *TV series* presenter Simon Callow pictured outside the Musikverein. Renowned for its acoustics, this concert hall is considered one of the finest in the world and is home to the Vienna Philharmonic Orchsestra. It was opened in January 1870.

LEFT: The interior of the Orangerie Schönbrunn which is the second largest orangery in Europe after the one at Versailles. Completed in 1755, it was here that Mozart participated in a conducting 'duel' with Antonio Salieri.

LUDWIG VAN BEETHOVEN AT A GLANCE

"Keep an eye on him; one day the he will make the world talk of him." Thus spoke an admiring Mozart after hearing Beethoven play the organ, aged just 17. Ludwig van Beethoven was born in the German city of Bonn on 16 December 1770. Both his father and grandfather were musicians at the Electorial chapel (the region of Beethoven's birth being administered by the Archbishop-Elector of Cologne). The lad displayed musical talent early on, but also apparently evident from a young age was the awkwardness and obstinacy that would see Ludvig continually branded as either "temperamental" or "difficult". In 1784, at the age of 14, he was appointed assistant organist at the Electoral chapel. His tuition in the instrument had been from Christian Gottlob Neefe, the great organist, who introduced Beethoven to Bach's *The Well-Tempered Klavier*. Neefe's recognition of the young man's abilities undoubted aided the appointment.

In 1787 Beethoven was sent to Vienna for further study, and during this visit he met Mozart. However, after only a short time in the Austrian city, the impending death of his mother compelled Beethoven to return to Bonn. Five years later he was back in Vienna, becoing a pupil of Joseph Haydn. By all reports the relationship was less than harmonious, but nevertheless, within a short time Beethoven became Vienna's most pre-eminent musician after Haydn and his output – primarily of chamber music – was considerable, including the *Pathétique* piano concerto.

Beethoven's first symphony was written in 1800 and, as any classical music lover knows, was followed by another eight – in 1802, 1803 (the *Eroica*), 1806, 1807, 1808 (number six, *The Pastoral*), 1812 (when both the seventh and eighth were written) and 1822 (the colossal and iconic *Choral*).

Around 1798, Beethoven first became aware of hearing problems which he initially hoped were temporary, but which, by 1800, were becoming progressively worse. For a time he withdrew from society, eventually being coaxed out or retirement by a lady friend, the Countess Giulietta Guicciardi, to whom he dedicated his *Sonata in C sharp minor*.

Beethoven's only opera, *Fidelio*, was composed in 1805 when he was at the height of his creative abilities. The first dozen years of the 19th century saw the production of many masterpieces – in addition to the symphonies, the *Mass in C*, the violin concerto, the *Coriolan* and *Egmont* overtures, the *Razoumovsky Quartets*, the *Emperor* piano concerto and numerous sonatas. Better was to come and, in his so-called "late period", Beethoven produced some of his greatest works – the *Piano Sonata in B flat*, the *Mass in D* (the *Missa Solemnis*) and the ninth symphony including a setting of Schiller's *Ode to Joy*.

In the last years of his life, now profoundly deaf, Beethoven became a recluse and, from 1825, his health began to fail. In early 1827 he contracted pneumonia which led to other complications and his death on 26 March.

Beethoven was enraged and ripped the title page from his work. It became known as *Eroica*, sub-titled "composed to celebrate the memory of a great man".

Sometime around 1802, Beethoven was forced to accept that his intermittent hearing problems would eventually lead to total deafness.

This realisation devastated him. Just outside Vienna, in a house in the village of Heiligenstadt, he wrote a letter to his brothers, telling of the pain he was enduring socially, psychologically and musically. The letter, now called the Heiligenstadt Testament, also helps to explain why Beethoven had a reputation for rudeness and irritability.

"Oh, how could I possibly admit an infirmity in the one sense which ought to be more perfect in me than in others, a sense which I once possessed in the highest perfection... oh, I cannot do it; therefore forgive me when you see me draw back when I would gladly have mingled with you."

Beethoven's works are divided into three chronological periods — early, middle and late. His hearing started deteriorating towards the end of the early period when he was writing most of his piano sonatas, the most famous being the *Pathétique* and the *Moonlight Sonata*. During the middle period, as his hearing grew worse, Beethoven's

work became more intense and emotional. It's during this time that he composed *Eroica* as well as the fifth and sixth symphonies, the fourth and fifth piano concertos and his sole opera, *Fidelio*. Beethoven's late period is marked by his total deafness and resulting isolation from the world, but it's now that many believe he reached his peak. He wrote the last of his great piano sonatas and string quartets, the *Missa solemnis* (Mass in D) and arguably his crowning glory, the *Symphony No. 9 in D minor*. When Beethoven first conducted this controversial symphony, he had to be turned around by one of the orchestra musicians to see the applause which he could not hear.

The composer whose work was almost synonymous with 19th century Vienna has to be Johann Strauss II. Known as 'The Waltz King', he was born in 1825, the first of five children. His father, Johann senior, was also a musician and composer of note, but actively dissuaded his sons from following in his footsteps. As it happens, all three — Johann, Josef and Eduard — become successful musicians. Young Johann was secretly encouraged by his mother to learn the violin and, at the age of six, he

Concert violinist and Classical Destinations *TV series co-presenter Niki Vasilakis plays in front of the monument to Johann Strauss II in Vienna's Stadtpark.*

made his first attempt at writing a waltz. Expelled from the school where he was studying accounting — for unspecified "misbehaviour" — Johann turned to studying music. On 15 October 1844 he performed in public for the first time, at the Dommayer Casino with his own orchestra playing his compositions.

Despite his father's opposition to his musical career, Johann maintained he was his inspiration. When Johann senior died, aged only 45, the younger Johann's career blossomed. A gilt statue of him in Vienna's Stadtplatz, on the Ringstrasse, bears testament to his place in classical music history.

During the summer Strauss had a full appointment book every night and while he lived to work, he was also renowned for throwing lively parties. He was good friends with Brahms, admired by Liszt and, by all reports, was idolised by women. In 1862 he secretly married an opera singer named Jetty Treffz. As Jetty already had seven children of her own — without ever marrying — the couple thought it better to face the

LEFT: The Zentralfriedhof (Central Cemetery) contains the graves of the composers Beethoven (left) and Schubert (right) as well as a monument to Mozart (centre). Both Brahms and Johan Strauss II are also buried here.

BELOW: The monument to Franz Liszt in the town of Eisenstadt. It was unveiled in 1936 to celebrate the 125th anniversary of the composer's birth.

gossip about their relationship after tying the knot. By all accounts it was a very happy marriage and the time they shared was Strauss' most prolific and successful. Notable works included *On The Beautiful Blue Danube* (1867), *Tales from the Vienna Woods* (1868) and, of course, *Die Fledermaus* (1874). Apparently it was Jetty who convinced Johann to compose operettas even though he was unsure of his talent in this area. He eventually wrote 15 of which *Die Fledermaus* is the best known. Just a year after it was premiered, it had been performed around the world and still is today.

After 15 years of marriage, Jetty died suddenly and Johann was so distraught he couldn't attend the funeral. Not long after, he threw himself into a disastrous second marriage to another singer, Lili Diettrich. It only lasted four years, and he was rescued from his despondency by the young and attractive Adele Deutsch, eventually marrying her. The climax of his career was a week-long festival staged in 1894 to celebrate the 50th anniversary of his debut at the casino. Tributes poured in from all over the world and, in a moving speech, he named the source of his inspiration,

"My beloved city Vienna, in whose soil is rooted my whole strength, in whose air floated the melodies my heart drank in and my hand wrote down."

Fifty kilometres southeast of Vienna is the town of Eisenstadt, capital of Austria's most easterly province. Burgenland was a part of Hungary from the mid-15th century until 1918 when the people voted to become part of the new Republic of Austria. Eisenstadt is situated on the southern slopes of the Leitha mountains, surrounded by vineyards. In the late 14th century the ruling family erected a fortified wall around the city and built a citadel inside it, creating the magnificent Schloss Esterházy.

Franz Joseph Haydn was born in Rohrau, Austria in 1732. He was the eldest son in a large Catholic family and, as such, would have been expected to become a priest. However, he had such a fine singing voice that, at the age of six, he was noticed by the Kapellmeister at St Stephen's Cathedral in Vienna. Shortly after, young Haydn was

The life and work of Johann Strauss II (also called 'Strauss the Younger') is celebrated in the Vienna home where he lived and composed his most famous work The Beautiful Blue Danube. *This violin is one of the many displays of Strauss memorabilia in what's now called* The Danube Waltz House.

enrolled in what is now known as the Vienna Boys Choir.

When his voice broke, Haydn was dismissed from the choir and pursued composing. He earned a living by teaching music, but was himself taught by the singer Nicola Porpora who helped develop his compositional skills. Largely self-taught, Joseph Haydn made a significant contribution to the classical style of composing which characterises the period from around 1750 to 1820. Often called the 'father of the symphony', Haydn was a major influence on Mozart and taught Beethoven in Vienna.

In 1759 he was appointed music director for Count Morzin in Bohemia and, after the performing of his first symphony, Haydn was approached by Prince Paul Anton Esterházy and asked to join the royal court in Eisenstadt as assistant *Kapellmeister*. The court boasted an orchestra, private theatre and chorus. Haydn remained there for 30 years during which time virtually all of his symphonies and operas were composed and performed. When he eventually left the Esterházy court in 1791 it was to move to England for the first of two 18-month residencies.

Haydn lived just five minute's walk from the palace in Eisenstadt. Today his home is, of course, a museum called the Haydnhaus (the Haydn House). He lived here from 1766 to 1778 with his wife, Maria Keller. The marriage was not a happy one. Haydn had been in love with Maria's younger sister, but that hadn't stopped her becoming a nun. They had no children, nor did they love each other. He once wrote to a friend in Vienna, saying that his letters comforted him and helped "…in my solitude… to cheer my heart, often so deeply hurt".

BELOW: The Esterházy Palace in Eisenstadt. The Esterházys were one of the wealthiest and most influential Hungarian families of the 18th century. Joseph Haydn worked for them for nearly 30 years from 1761.

FOLLOWING PAGES: During Haydn's time, the Esterházy Palace was very active musically with an orchestra, choir and solo singers. The palace's concert hall is pictured above.

FRANZ JOSEPH HAYDN AT A GLANCE

Unlike many of the great composers, Franz Joseph Haydn was not born into a musical family. His father was a wheelwright and the family, who lived in Rohrau in lower Austria, were poor and working class. Joseph was born on 31 March 1732 and was found to possess a beautiful singing voice, prompting the family to send him to his cousin, Johann Matthias Franck, for musical training. He came to the attention of the *kapellmeister* of St Stephen's Cathedral in Vienna, Karl Georg Reutter, who recruited him for the choir.

In 1748, when aged 15, Haydn's voice broke so he was dismissed from the choir. With no income, he turned to composing while also receiving some education from the Italian composer and singing teacher, Nicola Porpora. Haydn's talent for composing was evident early on in works including the Mass in F. In 1759 he was appointed *musik-direcktor* to Count Morzin's private orchestra and, for the first time, received a salary. After the orchestra disbanded in 1761, Haydn, was recruited by Prince Paul Anton Esterházy as *vizekapellmeister* to the court at Eisenstadt (then situated in Hungary). He remained with the wealthy and influential Esterházy family until 1790. Initially he was prevented from publishing his compositions outside the court, but from 1770 this restriction was lifted and Haydn quickly gained wider fame.

While visiting Vienna in late 1781 Haydn had his first meeting with Mozart and the two became good and mutually respectful friends. In 1785 Mozart composed a set of six quartets dedicated to Haydn. When Prince Nicholas - who had succeeded his brother in 1766 – himself died in 1790, the new prince promptly ceased all the palace's musical activities. Haydn left the court (incidentally, now a wealthy man) and went to London at the invitation of the impresario Johann Peter Salomon who had commissioned six symphonies. Haydn stayed in England for 18 months, enjoying huge success including the awarding of an honorary doctorate of music from Oxford University. On the journey back to Vienna in 1792, Haydn visited Bonn where he briefly met Beethoven who subsequently became his pupil. In 1794, Haydn visited England again for another 18-month stay, producing another six commissioned symphonies for J.P. Salomon. He again returned to Austria and the court of Esterházy, working for the grandson of Prince Nicholas, mainly composing masses and sacred music. During these latter years Haydn wrote his two great oratorios – *The Creation* (1798) and *The Seasons* (1801) – and what became the Austrian national anthem, the *Austrian Hymn* (1797).

When the French occupied Vienna in 1809, Haydn was a dying man so Napoleon ordered that his home be guarded and the composer left undisturbed. Franz Joseph Haydn died on 31 May 1809 and was buried in Vienna (the original gravestone remains in Haydn Park), but in 1954 the body was later moved to a dedicated mausoleum, paid for by the Esterházy family, in Eisenstadt's Bergkirche.

As an interesting aside, one of Haydn's brothers, Michael, was hired as conductor by the Prince-Archbishop of Salzburg and was also a friend of the Mozart family.

In 1790, after the death of Prince Nicolaus Esterházy, Haydn was free to travel and he accepted a lucrative commission to write and conduct six new symphonies in London. Before he left, Mozart is said to have asked Haydn, "How will you survive in London where you do not speak the language and people do not know you?"

He showed Mozart a card. "See this signature?" he replied. "That is all I need. The world knows my name!"

Haydn actually asked Mozart to go with him to London, as they were good friends, but Mozart declined as Constanze was ill. Mozart died the same year.

The concert season in London was a huge success and Haydn was given an honorary doctorate from Oxford University. When he returned, he lived in Vienna where he taught a promising young student called Ludwig van Beethoven. Much of Beethoven's work from this time exhibits Haydn's influence. In 1794 Haydn returned to England to produce another six symphonies, and the 12 works have since become collectively known as the 'London set'.

Haydn returned to the Esterházy court in Eisenstadt in 1795 where he composed mostly

church music, including six masses. He also wrote the music for Austria's national anthem. Haydn died in Vienna in May 1809 as Napoleon's army bombarded the city's gates. In 1820 the Prince returned the composer's remains to Eisenstadt where they were interned in the Bergkirche. While Haydn has important associations with other places it was his highly productive time at Eisenstadt which has since proved to be so significant in the evolution of classical music.

Scandinavia

Norway

…Once you see where Grieg lived,
you can understand how intrinsic the
feel of landscape is to his music. Hearing it,
you begin to imagine fjords and lakes, forests
full of trolls and goblins. Think of the famous
'Morning Mood' from his Peer Gynt music.
It's got that Nordic freshness stamped all over
it. You almost can taste the clean air
coming off the glacier…

Simon Callow

Olav Kyrre, but its harbour had been in use long before this. It became the largest town in the country and the capital of a region known as Norgesveldet which included Greenland, Iceland and even some of Scotland. Although Oslo became the Norwegian capital at the start of the 14th century, Bergen continued to grow and became a significant trading centre, especially during the medieval period of the Hanseatic League. The League comprised mainly German merchants and traded corn to Norway in return for fish.

Fishing was also the business of Alexander Greig who, in 1770, moved to Bergen from Scotland with his family. Alexander later changed the family name to Grieg. In June 1843, the great-grandson of Alexander Grieg was born in Bergen and became Norway's greatest composer, Edvard Hagerup Grieg.

In 2000, Bergen was named European City of Culture and at the Public Library, there is an extensive archive of Grieg memorabilia which includes everything from autographs through the account books he kept meticulously. The collection includes letters to his wife, originals of some compositions and even a 'musical greeting' from his friend, the German composer Johannes Brahms.

Edvard's mother, Gesine, was an accomplished pianist so a musical education was assured. Gesine was also active in the local music society as had been her parents. Founded in 1765, the society, or 'Harmonien', is one of the world's oldest orchestras. Today it's called the Bergen Philharmonic Orchestra and the magnificent Grieghallen, built at the end of the 1970s, is its home.

By all accounts Edvard was a fun-loving character. The family lived a long way from the school he attended so the journey was long and frequently undertaken in the rain. The young Grieg noticed that the pupils who arrived at school wet were sent home to change. As he lived a long distance from the school, this would effectively mean a day off. He took to exploiting the school's policy by standing under a gutter to make sure he was well and truly soaked when he arrived for class. One day he came unstuck when he turned up dripping wet even though it had hardly rained at all!

Edvard's musical potential was recognised by Ole Bull who was Norway's greatest violin virtuoso of the time. Born in Bergen in 1810, Bull gave concerts all over the world and was particularly successful in the USA where he attempted to set up a Norwegian community. Ole's brother was married to Edvard Grieg's aunt and this family link, as well as a shared

PREVIOUS PAGES: Views of the majestic Sognefjord, the deepest and longest fjord in the world.

INSET: Grieg's desk in his composers hut at Troldaugen.

ABOVE: The fish markets are considered to be the heart of Bergen.

OPPOSITE: An apple orchard at Lofthus, near Ullensvang. Grieg would have been inspired by this view when he went on walks from his summer house.

BERGEN AT A GLANCE

WEBSITE – www.visitBergen.com

COMPOSERS – Edvard Grieg, Ole Bull, Harald Sæverud.

Population – 237,000.

CLIMATE

WINTER – average temperature ranges from -2 to -7 degrees Celsius; typically around six hours of sunlight in mid-winter.

SPRING – average temperature is around 8 degrees Celsius; typically around 14 hours of sunlight by mid-spring.

SUMMER – average temperature is around 16 to 18 degrees Celsius; typically around 20 hours of sunlight in mid-summer.

AUTUMN – average temperature is around 8 to 9 degrees, typically around 11 hours of sunlight in mid-autumn.

BEST TIME OF THE YEAR TO VISIT – April to October.

TOP FIVE TOURIST ATTRACTIONS

BRYGGEN (the Wharf) – World Heritage listed, www.visitBergen.com

THE FISH MARKET – www.torgetibergen.no

FLØIBANEN FUNICULAR – www.floibanen.no

THE BERGEN AQUARIUM – www.akvariet.com

TROLDHAUGEN – Edvard Grieg's home for 53 years, www.troldhaugen.com

TOP TWO COFFEE HOUSES

Mr. Bean Coffee Shop, www.7nights.no

Baker Brun, www.bakerbrun.no

MUST SEE SHOPPING LOCATIONS

BRYGGEN AREA – souvenir shops.

SHOPPING CENTRES – Galleriet, Kløverhuset and Bergen Storsenter.

SMALL AND SPECIALISED SHOPS – Øvregaten, Lille Øvregate, Vetrlidsallmenning, Vågsallmenning, Strandkaien, Strandgaten and the area around the main square Torgallmenningen.

COMPOSERS MUSEUMS /HOMES

TROLDHAUGEN – the home of Noway's best

known composer, Edward Grieg, is now a museum, comprising an exhibition centre with a shop and cafe, concert hall and his composer's hut.

SILJUSTØL – the home of Harald Sæverud, one of the most important Norwegian composers of the 20th century.

LYSØEN ISLAND – the beautiful and extraordinary villa on Lysøen (the 'Island of Light') was built in 1873 as a summer residence for the Norwegian violin virtuoso Ole Bull.

GARDENS/PARKS MUST SEE

Arboretum And Botanical Garden at Milde – founded in 1971, the Arboretum occupies an area of 125 acres, part of which is planted with a variety of 'foreign' trees and shrubs.

Byparken – comprises the area around Lille Lungegårdsvann and contains fountain, a music pavilion and statues.

Lysøen Island (Ole Bull's Island) – this 175 acre island has around 13 kilometres of paths, ponds and gazebos.

Bryggeparken – this park contains the old 'cabbage patches' which were situated behind the Schøtstuene assembly rooms and the bakehouses.

Alvøen Country Mansion – dating from 1797, the mansion was the residence of the Fasmer family and is surrounded by a charming garden and park.

ANNUAL MUSICAL EVENTS

January – 'Ride This Train' – music festival, www.ridethistrain.no

April to May –Spring recitals at Siljustøl, www.siljustol.no

April – Bergen Music Fest – Ole Blues, www.bergenfest.no

May – Night Jazz, Jazz Festival, www.nattjazz.no

May – Bergen International Festival, www.festspillene.no

June to August – Summer concerts at Troldhaugen, www.troldhaugen.com

July to August – 'Grieg in Bergen' , www.musicanord.no

July – The Bergen Story, classical music concerts, www.musicanord.no

August – 'Lost Weekend' music festival, www.lost-weekend.net

August – Outdoor performances of the opera Aida, www.operabergen.no

September – Grieg Intenational Choir Festival, www.griegfestival.no

September to October – Autumn recitals at Troldhaugen, www.troldhaugen.com

September – Church Music Festival, www.bkf.no

November – 'Days of Church Music', www.bkf.no

November – National Music Competition, www.hulen.no

December – The Holberg Days, Baroque Music Festival, www.uib.no/griaka

INFORMATION

Tourist Information Centre, Vagsallmennigen 1, N-5014 Bergen, telephone +47 55 55 20 00, www.visitBergen.com

love of music, ensured a strong friendship developed between the violinist and Edvard's parents.

Sometime in 1858, Ole Bull visited the Griegs at their estate to hear Edvard play. Then just 15, the composer later described this day as the most important day in his life. After Edvard had played a number of his own compositions, Ole Bull first spoke quietly to the boy's parents, then turned to him and announced, "You are going to Leipzig to become an artist!"

That same year Grieg went to Germany where he studied at the Leipzig Conservatory — which had been founded by Felix Mendelssohn in 1842 — remaining there for five years before moving to Copenhagen. Here he encountered another young

ABOVE: Grieg and his wife built a summer house at Troldsalen, just south of Bergen. BELOW: In the 13th century Bergen was Norway's first capital, and was the country's largest city until 1830.

Norwegian composer, Rikard Nordraak, who was passionate about promoting Scandinavian composers and music. The two became firm friends, and Nordraak's patriotism (his music is used in the modern Norwegian national anthem) greatly influenced Grieg to begin pursuing Norwegian themes — from literature, folk music and dance — in his own work. Grieg later said of his friend, "He opened my eyes to the important in music that isn't music".

While in Copenhagen, Edvard met somebody else who was to become very important in his life. Nina Hagerup was his first cousin and the pair had actually grown up together in Bergen before she moved to Copenhagen with her family. After becoming re-acquainted, Edvard and Nina fell in love. She possessed a beautiful singing voice and when they were engaged in the spring of 1865, Grieg's present to Nina was four songs called *Melodies of the Heart*. The words were written by another friend — Hans Christian Andersen. Edvard and Nina were married in June 1867, but neither family approved nor attended the wedding. By all accounts Edvard and Nina were very much in love, but in spite of this, Nina's mother wasn't at all pleased. She is quoted as saying, "He has nothing! He cannot do anything and he makes music no one cares to listen to!"

It's true that, like so many composers, Grieg wasn't very popular at home. In fact, early on he struggled to make ends meet. In 1866 Edvard and Nina had moved to Oslo where they wanted to build a home for Norway's music in Norway's capital.

ABOVE: Grieg's composer's hut at 'Troldhaugen' overlooks the Grimstadfjorden and provided the solitude needed to write music.

FOLLOWING PAGES: The beautiful Troldsalen Concert Hall seats 200 and is set in the grounds of 'Troldhaugen', overlooking Grieg's beloved composer's hut.

ABOVE LEFT: *The interior of the hut at 'Troldhaugen' is as much as Grieg would have left it, with family pictures and music scores still in place. ABOVE CENTRE: Grieg was a short man so he had to sit on a collection of Beethoven's works in order to reach the keyboard. ABOVE RIGHT: A framed photograph of Grieg's wife Nina with the couple's daughter Alexandria. BELOW: Grieg's piano in the drawing room.*

Oslo is the modern capital of Norway and, in Grieg's time, it was known as Christiania (after King Christian IV). Like Bergen, Oslo is a very old city, founded in 1048 by King Harald Hardråde. Full of museums, galleries, parks, a royal palace and a castle built in the 1300s to guard the entrance to the harbour, it's a city built for people. Virtually all the attractions around the city can be reached on foot. Originally called Oslo, the city reverted back to this name in 1925.

Edvard and Nina's time in Christiania was hard; musically, financially and personally. To scrape together a living, Edvard taught piano and conducted. His good friend Rikard Nordraak died of tuberculosis aged only 24 and this had a profound affect on Grieg. In 1868 their fortunes began to change — the Griegs' daughter Alexandra was born and it also was the year Edvard wrote the majestic and popular *Piano Concerto in A minor*. However, the following year, barely six weeks after the successful premiere of the piano concerto in Copenhagen, Alexandra died of meningitis (incidentally, while the family was visiting Bergen). After her death, Edvard and Nina had no more children.

In 1870 Edvard travelled to Rome where he met the Hungarian composer Franz Liszt. This meeting proved to be the turning point for Grieg. Reportedly Liszt played Grieg's piano concerto by sight and was greatly impressed. As Liszt was the 'grand old man' of music at the time, his approval and encouragement was of enormous value to Grieg's musical future. In 1875 he completed the *Peer Gynt* suites, based on a poem by Ibsen largely derived from Norwegian fairy tales. The suit comprises eight pieces, the three best known being *Morning Mood, In the Hall of the Mountain King* and *Solveig's Song*.

OPPOSITE: It's easy to see how the spectacular Norwegian scenery inspired much of Grieg's music.

ABOVE: The Flåm to Myrdal railway is one of the steepest in the world, climbing to 866 metres above sea level in 20 kilometres. For the return journey, the train employs five sets of brakes.

EDVARD GRIEG AT A GLANCE

Of Scottish descent, Edvard Grieg was born in the Norwegian city of Bergen on 15 June 1843. He was first taught piano by his mother and composed his first piece for the instrument when aged nine. At 15 Edvard was sent to study music in Leipzig where he was influenced by the works of Schumann.

After moving to Copenhagen in 1863, Grieg started to develop an interest in music based on Scandinavian – and, more specifically, Norwegian – folk songs, poems and legends. This interest was shared with another Norwegian composer, Rikard Nordraak, whose death at just 24 spurred Grieg to dedicate his life to the promotion of Nordic music.

While in Rome in 1865, he met the Norwegian playwright Henrik Ibsen who asked the composer to write some incidental music for his play *Peer Gynt* (itself based on Norwegian fairy tales). Grieg found the project a challenge which took many years to complete to his satisfaction, but it helped establish him as one of the 19th century's key composers.

In 1866 Grieg returned to Norway, settling in Christiania (now Oslo) and, a year later, marrying his cousin Nina Hagerup. A talented singer, she helped popularise many of his songs. In early 1869 Grieg received a letter from Franz Liszt who, after hearing the Norwegian's *Sonata for Violin and Piano in F*, wanted to meet him. The two met in Rome and Liszt played the newly published *Piano Concerto in A minor* in its entirety by sight-reading.

As the result of severe pleurisy at the age of 17, Grieg suffered from fragile health throughout his life, but this didn't stop him embarking on gruelling concert tours through Europe every year. On these tours he met and became friends with many of his contemporaries including Tchaikovsky, Brahms, Delius and Saint-Saëns.

In 1784 he was awarded a grant by the Norwegian government which enabled him to settle in his country of birth. He built a house on Bergen's Hardanger Fjord which he called 'Troldhaugen', and also a composer's hut overlooking the water with a view to the majestic mountains that were often his inspiration. The last 20 years of his life were spent composing at Troldhaugen, although he was constantly afflicted by ill-health which caused great frustration.

Nevertheless Grieg continued to conduct concert tours throughout Europe, leaving Norway each year during the winter months. It was while preparing to travel to a music festival in the English city of Leeds, that Grieg's poor health and a life of hard work finally took their toll. He died in Bergen's hospital on 4 September 1907 and was buried at Troldhaugen.

As well as successfully expressing the spirit of his native country in music, Edvard Grieg became an important influence on other composers of the early 20th century, including Bela Bartók, Maurice Ravel and Claude Debussy.

On the Sognefjord's innermost branches, small villages and farms cling tenaciously to the steep sides of the gorges. Heavy snowfalls during winter have dictated sturdy building designs using logs and stone. ABOVE: These details are from the village of Otternes, not far from Flåm, which includes a preserved 18th century farm. BELOW: Two views from the Flåm to Myrdal railway.
OPPOSITE: The village of Otternes.

WEBSITES — www.alr.no, www.visitflam.com

COMPOSERS — The village of Flåm isn't known for any composers, but there's no doubt Edvard Grieg would have enjoyed the spectacular scenery. He may well have visited the area like many other painters, writers and members of the European Royal families.

POPULATION — Small village with only 450 inhabitants.

CLIMATE

WINTER - cool to cold climate, but low snowfall; temperature range of 5 to -10 degrees Celsius.

SPRING - mild, temperature range of 12 to 18 degrees Celsius.

SUMMER - warm and sunny, temperature range of 18 to 22 degrees Celsius.

Autumn — mild with beautiful colours, temperature range of 12 to 18 degrees Celsius.

BEST TIME OF THE YEAR TO VISIT: May to June and August to September.

TOP FIVE TOURIST ATTRACTIONS

THE FLÅM RAILWAY
The Flåm Railway is one of the most famous and spectacular train journeys in the world. A masterpiece of engineering, there is no other railway in the world running on normal tracks that is so steep over such a long distance; 20 kilometres with a rise of 865 metres. www.flaamsbana.no

The Flåm Railway Documentation Centre

The Documentation Centre gives you an insight in to the building of the world's steepest railway, the technical development and the people behind this unique engineering project. The centre has displays showing the history and everyday life in Flåm, and train operations on the Bergen Railway. www.flaamsbana.no

OTTERNES FARM MUSEUM
This historic farm consists of 27 buildings in a cluster with an impressive view of the Sognefjord. These buildings are mostly log houses and preserved as they where in the 18th century. In addition, the old cultural landscape with hills, wells, stairs and stone structure is still intact. Today Otternes is a centre for old handcraft techniques and traditional Norwegian cuisine. www.otternes.no

UNDREDAL
Undredal is a charming village on the Aurlandsfjord with just 130 inhabitants... and some 500 goats! Enjoy the many hiking trails in the mountains or visit 'The House Of Cheese'. A guided tour of Scandinavia's smallest stave church at Aurland is highly recommended. Dating from 1147, the church contains original decorations from the 15th century. www.alr.no

MAGICAL WHITE CAVES OF GUDVANGEN
The high mountains that surround Gudvangen hide a secret. Inside the mountain are large quantities of pure anorthosite. A type of marble, this mineral is use for cleaning toxic industrial material and is exported to all over Europe. Today one of the mines has been converted into an interactive and spiritual art experience, combining sounds and silence, light and music (including Grieg's Hall of the Mountain King). The experience is tailored for groups and the minimum number accepted is 20. www.gudvangen.com

TOP TWO COFFEE HOUSES

Fretheim Hotel — coffeebar telephone (+47) 57 63 63 00, fax (+47) 57 63 64 00, www.fretheim-hotel.no

Furukroa — telephone (+47) 57 63 20 50, fax (+47) 57 63 20 51, www.furukroa.no

MUST SEE SHOPPING LOCATIONS

Souvenir shops in the village centre.

GARDENS/PARKS MUST SEE

Enjoy the beautiful scenery that surrounds the village. There are a number of marked hiking trials.

BELOW: The village of Lofthus is on the Sørfjorden, about two-and-a-half hours east of Bergen. Grieg was so inspired by the area he had a small composer's hut built which today is in the grounds of the Hotel Ullensvang.

While his fame as a composer grew, Grieg's personal life wasn't going so well. His parents died in 1875 and, a few year's later, Edvard left Nina. However, his increased popularity in the musical world, and the awarding of an artist's grant, meant Grieg no longer needed to either teach or conduct. He began extensive tours through Europe — to Leipzig, Berlin, Prague, London and Paris — travelling during the cooler months and returning to Norway for the summer. By now, though, Edvard was

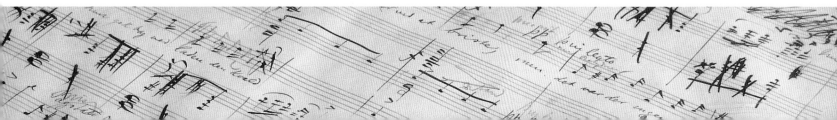

ABOVE: Oslo's Royal Palace – Det Kongelige Slottet – is where Norway's National Day celebrations (held on 7 May) are centred each year.

RIGHT: In the late 19th century the Norwegian artist Edvard Munch depicted Oslo as a city inhabited by the "living dead"! Today it is a much more vibrant and colourful place which celebrates a history of over a thousand years.

OPPOSITE: The Vigeland Sculpture Park is a not far from Oslo's city centre. It occupies 80 acres and contains a remarkable 212 statues by the Norwegian sculptor Gustav Vigeland who spent 36 years, between 1906 and 1942, creating the park.

struggling with depression. He was persuaded by a friend, Frantz Beyer, to reconcile with Nina and in 1885 the couple reunited.

On a hill five kilometres south of Bergen is 'Troldhaugen', the summer house built by the reconciled Edvard and Nina and where they spent the last 22 years of their lives together. Today it is a museum dedicated to the composer and the house is much as he left it with manuscripts still piled on his piano. The beautiful Troldsalen Concert Hall was built on the property in 1985, overlooking Grieg's beloved composer's hut. Concerts are regularly held in the hall during summer, once again blending music and scenery.

Fjords are an integral part of the Norwegian landscape. During the last ice age, glaciers scoured deep valleys and, as the ice receded, the melt water continued to shape the land. The Sognefjord is the longest in the world and also the deepest, in places up to 1300 metres deep (over 4200 feet). At the head of a branch of the Sogne, called the Aurlandfjord, is the village of Flåm.

The Fretheim Hotel in Flåm was first built in 1870 and, even though it has been refurbished and enlarged a number of times over the years, still

preserves its traditional heritage. Surrounded by steep mountainsides, roaring waterfalls and deep valleys, the Fretheim Hotel is in a paradise.

The Flåm railway is a one-of-a-kind experience. It's a branch line from the main Bergen to Oslo track, but is worth every second of the 60 minutes it takes from Flåm to where it joins the main line at Myrdal. The railway is one of the steepest in the world. In 20 kilometres it goes from sea level to Myrdal at 866 metres (2857 feet) above sea level. The tunnels weave through the mountains, at one point doing a full 180 degree turn inside the mountain. Even though the train crosses the river three times, there are no bridges. Instead the river is fed through the mountains by a system of tunnels under the railway.

The Hotel Ullensvang on the Sørfjorden, is about a two-and-a-half hour's drive from Bergen. It was built in 1846 and has been run by the Utne family for four generations. The whole region around the hotel and the little village of Lofthus is beautiful. In spring, the slopes are covered in fruit blossoms. It's no surprise that Edvard Grieg found this area especially inspiring. He first came here in 1877 and had a small composer's hut built.

Locals called the cabin 'Komposten' — the compost — which Grieg didn't appreciate much. Nor did he welcome their interruptions when he was working there so he insisted it was moved, with the help of local farmers, down to the seashore. Three years later Grieg sold the hut and years later it was discovered on an island about 150 kilometres away, being used as a chicken coop. It was moved back to its original location on the banks of the fjord at Lofthus where today it's part of the Hotel Ullensvang with stunning views of the fjord which so inspired the composer.

Towards the end of his life Edvard Grieg was in great demand, travelling constantly while also continuing to write songs, piano pieces and other music. This heavy workload eventually got the better of him, exacerbated by a lung condition he had struggled with since childhood. In September 1907, while preparing for a trip to England, he collapsed. A few days later he died in Bergen Hospital from chronic exhaustion. At his request, Edvard was cremated and his ashes inserted into the rock face at his beloved 'Troldhaugen'. When Nina passed away many years later, her ashes were added to the gravesite.

Grieg loved Norway and became passionate about representing his country in his music. He chose not to follow the influences of earlier composers and instead turned to Norway's traditions and landscape to develop a nationalistic style. He is quoted as saying, "Artists like Bach and Beethoven erected churches and temples on the heights. I only wanted to build dwellings for men in which they might feel happy and at home".

ABOVE: Edvard Grieg's ashes are interned in a rock face at his beloved 'Troldhaugen'.

OPPOSITE ABOVE: At Undredal, on the Aurlandfjord branch, is the smallest church in Scandinavia, dating back to 1147.

OPPOSITE BELOW: The Sognefjord is the longest and deepest fjord in the world. It stretches 200 kilometres and is 1300 metres deep. This dramatic landscape was shaped during the Ice Age as glaciers carved the steep gorges.

Finland

Helsinki
Rovaniemi

*…Sibelius' music sounds
as if it has been exhaled from the earth
and blown directly into our ears from those
ancient Finnish forests and frozen lakes.
People recognised this quality as soon
as Sibelius burst onto the scene as
a young man in the 1890s…*

SIMON CALLOW

Finland is a land of extremes. Even in midsummer, when people are at the harbour beaches in Helsinki, north in Lapland, it can be snowing. Nearly 80 percent of Finland is either water or forest. The country has a population of 5.2 million, 20 percent of whom live in the Helsinki metropolitan area. Finland's capital city is a magical blend of art and nature. It's is a good-natured city — small enough to not have to grapple with issues of pollution and traffic jams, but big enough to have significant culture and entertainment possibilities.

The Finnish National Opera is known around the world and has had its home at the Helsinki Opera House since the building was opened in 1993. Much Finnish and international opera is performed here, as well as ballets and other concerts. The extremes of climate is one of the reasons why the Finns are so good at doing things indoors. The Helsinki Museum of Modern Art is called the Kiasma. Part living room, part cultural centre and part museum, it was opened in 1998.

Helsinki is also a trading port. From here ships travel back and forth to other Baltic ports, thence around the world. Because of the importance of trade, Helsinki's harbour is vital. In winter, icebreakers work constantly to keep it open.

In recent years, Finland has moved ahead significantly and is home to one of the leading companies in mobile phone technology. Though the name sounds Asian to western ears, Nokia is actually a Finnish company named after the town of Nokia, about an hour or so north-west of Helsinki. The name "Nokia" derives from the old Finnish word for a black-furred sable.

A renowned institution in Helsinki is the Hotel Kämp. It was completed in 1887 and, in the words of its own publicity brochures, "...the Kämp has a great many stories to tell".

Over the past 100 years or so, the fates of the Hotel Kämp and Finland have been closely knit together. The restaurants in the hotel have provided a beautiful setting for fabulous parties. The identity of the emerging Finnish nation was blueprinted at the Kämp. Important political issues have been decided and significant deals closed at its tables.

The Kämp has had a varied history. At one point in the middle of last century, it was doubtful that the old place would survive. But survive it has and, under the present owners, has been faithfully and painstakingly restored to many of its original specifications. However, an old building is just an old building without the history of the lives which passed through, and one such life was the most famous of Finnish composers — Jean Sibelius.

PREVIOUS PAGES: Lapland is Finland's northern most province and much of it is north of Arctic Circle, so during summer, the sun doesn't set for early 70 days. For this reason, Lapland has been called 'the land of the midnight sun'.

A detail of the monument in Helsinki's Sibelius Park which is dedicated to Finland's most famous classical composer. INSET: The reindeer farm at Rovaniemi in Lapland.

ABOVE: A market stall holder takes advantage of a great harbour front location at the markets in Helsinki.

OPPOSITE: Helsinki was founded on a site at the head of the Vantaa River in 1550 by King Gustav Vasa. His aim was to develop a harbour to rival that of Tallin in Estonia.

TOP AND ABOVE: The Hotel Kämp was a favourite drinking hole for Jean Sibelius. It's said that on occasion his wife, Aino, had to send local men to the hotel to bring Jean home after a drinking session.

Johan Julius Christian Sibelius was born in Hämeenlinna (which was then known by its Swedish name of Tavastehus), about 100 kilometres north of Helsinki, on 8 December 1865. His dissolute, alcoholic father died when he was two, leaving the rest of the family — himself, elder sister and young pregnant mother Maria Charlotta — with a mountain of debt. They went to live with Maria Charlotta's mother, having lost all but a few of their earthly possessions to bankruptcy.

At the time, Finland was part of the Russian Empire and was divided into two distinct classes of the educated and the uneducated. Most formal education was in Swedish. Fortunately for young Jean, this was his native language, but a change was in the air and, in 1873, the first Finnish language school in his home town opened its doors. His mother, in a moment of foresight, enrolled him. This was very important for Sibelius as it exposed him to the world of Finnish mythology which fired his imagination and proved to be foundational for much of his later work.

About 30 years before Sibelius was born, a group of traditional Finnish folk songs and poems were collected into one volume called the *Kalevala*. At the Ateneum — Helsinki's Museum of Art — there are a number of works based around the *Kalevala*. The richness of this literature and its pathos were transformed by Sibelius into a five-movement symphonic poem based on Kullervo... a boy whose tale is the saddest of all the *Kalevala* legends. Kullervo never succeeded at anything yet he was a boy consumed by revenge for the dreadful wrongs committed against his family. He lived a short life, wasted on hatred.

WEBSITE: www.helsinki.fi

COMPOSERS: Jean Sibelius. Einojuhani Rautavaara

POPULATION: 559,330.

CLIMATE

WINTER — average temperatures range from -5.0 to zero degrees Celsius. Around six hours of daylight. Snow and ice.

SPRING — average temperatures range from 1.0 to 5.0 degrees Celsius.

SUMMER — summer temperatures can exceed 20 degrees Celsius with up to 18 hours of daylight in mid-summer.

AUTUMN — average temperatures range from 5.0 to 10 degrees Celsius, and autumn is typically wet.

BEST TIME OF THE YEAR TO VISIT: Helsinki is an all-year-round destination, but spring to autumn is best for cultural events and December is recommended for Christmas concerts in churches and other celebrations.

TOP FIVE TOURIST ATTRACTIONS

LINNANMÄKI — a traditional funfair and one of the most popular attractions in Finland, www.linnanmaki.fi

SUOMENLINNA — a literal translation is "Finland's Castle", and it consists of five islands in Helsinki's harbour on which are spread ruined fortifications. www.suomenlinna.fi

TEMPPELIAUKION KIRKKO (The Church In The Rock) — a modern church built into solid rock and crowned with a copper dome. The walls have been left as unfinished rock. At Lutherinkatu 4.

KORKEASAARI-ZOO — Helsinki's zoo is located on Korkeasaari, one of the many islands in the city's harbour, www.korkeasaari.fi

USPENSKIN KATEDRAALI (Upensky Cathedral) — Russian Orthodox church built in 1868 with distinctive onion-shaped domes.

TOP TWO COFFEE HOUSES

Café Ekberg — www.cafeekberg.fi

Fazer Café — www.fazercafe.fi

MUST SEE SHOPPING LOCATIONS

Pohjoisesplanadi and Eteläesplanadi — main shopping thoroughfares in central Helsinki.

Aleksanterinkatu — known as 'Aleksi' for short and also in central Helsinki.

Kauppatori (Market Square) — souvenirs and local crafts as well as places to eat.

Akateeminen Kirjakauppa — Scandinavia's largest bookshop.

COMPOSERS MUSEUMS/HOMES

Ainola — Sibelius's summer home and museum in Järvenpää, around 45 kilometres from Helsinki (open summer months only).

Sibelius Home Museum — the birth place of the composer in Hämeenlinna and which includes his upright piano. Also used for occasional recitals.

GARDENS/PARKS MUST SEE

KAIVOPUISTO-PARK ON SEURASAARI ISLAND — in summer this parks is also an outdoor museum, www.nba.fi/fi/seurasaari

Esplanadin puisto (Esplanade Park) — a long, narrow city park which dates from

KASVITIETEELLINEN PUUTARHA (University Botanical Gardens) — central city gardens designed in the 1830s.

SIBELIUKSEN PUISTO (Sibelius Park) — park dedicated to the composer and includes a dramatic monument of welded steel pipes by the Finnish sculptor Eila Hiltunen, created in the early 1960s.

THE CITY WINTER GARDEN — established in 1893 to house hot-climate plants including palms and cacti. At Hammarkjöldintie 1.

ANNUAL MUSICAL EVENTS

August/September — Helsingin juhlaviikot (Helsinki Festival); music, theatre, dance, visual arts, film and other cultural events. www.helsinginjuhlaviikot.fi

INFORMATION

Helsinki Information Office and the City Tourist Board, first floor, Pohjoisesplanadi

Jean, however, was not like this. One of his school friends has left us a beautiful rendering of his character. A dreamer with a passionate love for nature and an extraordinary imagination, Jean was also given to sudden changes of mood, from excitable play to deep melancholy.

It seems he had a gentle heart and an affectionate nature. He was not brilliant academically, but he had a passion for music and played the violin admirably.

In 1885, Jean Sibelius finished school and went to Helsinki to study law. He enrolled at the Helsinki Music Institute — which is now the Sibelius Academy — and within a very short time his legal studies faded from view. Though he dreamt of a career as a violin virtuoso, Sibelius' time here convinced him that his future was in composition rather than performance. In 1889, his first masterpiece — the *String Quartet in A Minor* — was performed.

Sibelius continued his studies in Berlin and Vienna where he made his first sketches of the symphonic poem *Kullervo*. In the spring of 1892 he conducted it for the first time in Helsinki. It was a resounding success and began Sibelius' career as an orchestral composer and conductor.

The next year he finished another orchestral work, *En Saga*, and, in 1895, the *Lemminkäinen Suite*. The success of *Kullervo* was very important. With its traditional folk foundation, it gave strength to the growing sense of nationalism in Finland. Its success also helped quiet the doubts of his

prospective in-laws about their daughter marrying a musician. In June 1892, Jean Sibelius married Aino Järnefelt in her parents' home and with that, became a part of one of the most aristocratic and well-known Finnish-speaking families.

He began to live at a frenetic pace. When he wasn't composing or conducting, he was teaching, playing chamber music or indulging in life's 'finer things'. The Hotel Kämp was one of his favourite watering holes.

However, Jean inherited some unfortunate traits from his father. One was the habit of spending money carelessly and the other was a propensity for heavy drinking. In the Hotel Kämp is the Jean Sibelius room, named in his honour, and it's probably quite fitting that this is where cocktail parties are now held.

Jean couldn't have been an easy person to live with. He was prone to dark depression and was sometimes gone for days drinking. Aino would sometimes have to send some of the local men out to bring him home from the Hotel Kämp.

Sibelius had six daughters, one of whom — Kirsti — died of typhoid as an infant. Despite the trials and the fact that there wasn't much money until later, Aino loved and understood Jean very well. From the time they were married in 1892, the couple lived in about ten different places in Helsinki and nearby Kerava, not to mention the summers spent with friends and Jean's long travels abroad for concert tours. But friends began to urge Jean, for the sake of his music and, most likely, his health to turn his back on the temptations of the city.

Sibelius himself felt the need for distance and peace. Nature and the woods influenced his writing enormously. He said, "In Helsinki, the song died within me". So, in 1904, the family moved into a house at Järvenpää, about an hour north of Helsinki. The house was called 'Ainola' in honour of Jean's long-suffering wife. Much of the design work for the house and ancilliary buildings was her's. The sauna, for example, was built according to Aino's designs.

OPPOSITE: Helsinki at sunset. Today the city is home to around 600,000 residents.

BELOW: The centre of Helsinki is served by a tram network which makes it easy for the tourist to get around.

ABOVE: Sibelius's piano, given to him on his 50th birthday, at his home 'Ainola' in Järvenpää which is around 45 kilometres from Helsinki. He lived here for 53 years.

OPPOSITE: Today, 'Ainola' is a museum, but the home is just as it was left after Jean's wife, Aino, died in 1969 (12 years after her husband).

The furnishings in the drawing room at 'Ainola' have remained virtually unchanged since it was converted from a studio in 1911. Some of the works of art are very precious indeed, including one depicting Aino, in the 1880s, on the rocks by the seashore before she was engaged to Jean. It was painted by her brother Eero Järnefelt.

The drawing room resonates with memories. Jean and Aino's youngest daughter, Heidi, made the ceramic vases on display. She was quite an accomplished ceramicist and earned a bronze medal for her work at the Paris World's Fair of 1937. Heidi died in 1982.

Jean and Aino's oldest daughter, Eva, said of her childhood at 'Ainola', "When we children were small, it seemed to us that 'Ainola', our home, was a ship on the wide seas and nothing was safe or certain outside it".

Her feeling that way was understandable. The outside world was not altogether safe. Finland was, at that time, an autonomous Grand Duchy ruled by the Tsar of Russia. From 1899 on, a period of resistance and social upheaval began in Finland which culminated in its declaration of independence in 1917 — the same year, of course, as the Russian Revolution.

Though the declaration was final, the process was gradual. Finland acquired its own National Parliament in 1906, elected by equal and universal suffrage, which makes Finnish women the first in the world to be granted full national political rights.

'Ainola' was a place of tranquillity and creativity for Jean. Most of his work was written in the dining room which would have seen many an interesting discussion. An interesting question from their daughters might have been, "Papa, if your name is Johan, why does everyone call you Jean?".

Sibelius had an uncle Johan who died about a year before he was born. One day, as a small boy, he was playing with some of the things his uncle had left behind. He found a packet of calling cards — business cards as they're known today. As his uncle was a sailor and travelled widely, he had used the French version of his name — Jean — on the cards. Young Sibelius kept them and, 20 years later, introduced them as his own… and the name stuck.

FOLLOWING PAGES: Views from around 'Ainola'. Sibelius selected this location for its peace and tranquillity… he liked to compose in complete silence.

'Ainola', the house Sibelius and his wife

Aino created, is an unpretentious sort of a dacha

in the countryside only a few miles from the city,

but deep in the heart of nature.

ABOVE: *The reindeer farm at Rovaniemi. The reindeer 'wrangler' is dressed in traditional Sámi costume. Rovaniemi is very close to the Arctic Circle.*

OPPOSITE: *Pine forest at the edge of Helsinki's airport... you're introduced to Finland's landscape the moment you arrive.*

The year 1908 was not a good one for Jean Sibelius. He was frequently sick and depressed along with it. Doctors found a malignant tumour in his throat which had probably been caused by his excessive drinking. After it had been operated on, the doctors warned him that he must stop smoking and drinking. It worked. What his wife and daughters had been trying to do for years, the threat of dying finally succeeded in achieving, and he gave up for eight years.

Sibelius was afraid dying and this is reflected in his music. His *Symphony no. 4 in A minor* is dark and brooding — full of depression — and it received a lot of negative criticism. Sibelius had a friend and patron by the name of Axel Carpelan who championed his cause and was the first to speak publicly in understanding of the "difficult language" of the fourth symphony. At one time, Carpelan rescued Sibelius from almost certain financial ruin. When he died in 1919, Sibelius lost a great friend and wrote in his diary, "For whom will I compose now?"

A frequent theme of Sibelius' music is the contrast between the harshness of a long, bitter winter and a brief but brilliant summer. Nowhere is this contrast more extreme than in Finland's north which forms part of Lapland, along with the higher latitudes of Norway and Sweden and into Russia. The Sámi people are native to this region. They used to be called Lapps, but this is now considered derogatory by many Sámi. In Finland, you're only accepted as Sámi if you can show that at least your grandparents spoke the Sámi language. In other Scandinavian countries, the criteria are different. In Sweden, for example, you only have to look after a herd of reindeer to be considered Sámi!

JEAN SIBELIUS AT A GLANCE

Like Edvard Grieg in Norway, Jean Sibelius was dedicated to exploring – through his music - themes derived from the mythology, literature and landscapes of his native Finland. However, his ability as a composer of symphonic music, in particular, gained him international claim.

Born Johan Julius Christian Sibelius on 18 December 1865 in the western Finnish town of Hämeenlinna, the name 'Jean' was adopted from a sea-farer uncle who used the French version of 'Johan' when he travelled overseas. Finland was then part of Tsarist Russia and ruled by a Swedish-speaking minority, but Finnish nationalism was beginning to emerge as Sibelius was growing up. He was enrolled in the country's first Finnish-speaking school, but didn't become proficient in the language until an adult. Sibelius initially studied law, but abandoned this subject in favour of music, studying under Martin Wegelius.

After periods in Berlin and Vienna, he returning to Finland in 1892 and, in the same year, produced his first major orchestral work. The five-movement *Kullervo Symphony* is based on a character from Finnish mythology and its first performance made Sibelius a local success. A commission from Finland's leading conductor of the time, Robert Kajanus, led to *En Saga*, another symphonic poem. Sibelius's best known work, *Finlandia*, was written in 1899 as music to accompany a series of patriot tableaux. In the same year, his *Symphony No.1* (the first of seven) brought international recognition.

Despite his growing international fame and increasing productivity, Sibelius remained debt-ridden and had a fondness for alcohol and cigars which caused health problems in later life. In 1904, he left Helsinki for a refuge he had built by the lake at Järvenpää, and called 'Ainola' (after his wife Aino). Sibelius lived here for the next 53 years until his death in 1957, and around 150 works were produced in the composer's hut overlooking the fjord. Likened to Mahler in terms of the majesty of his orchestration, Sibelius met the German composer when he visited Helsinki in 1907. Despite deteriorating health, Sibelius still travelled extensively, visiting France, Italy, Germany and England to conduct his works. A visit to the USA in 1914 culminated in an honorary doctorate from Yale University.

In 1918, following the 'October Revolution' in Russia, Finland declared independence, but a civil war ensued and Sibelius was forced to flee, for a short time, to Vienna. After the war, he completed his sixth (1923) and seventh (1924) symphonies and the symphonic poem *Tapiola* (1926), based on another theme from the mythological *Kalevala* which had earlier inspired *Kullervo*. There was an eighth symphony, but Sibelius was unhappy with the work and elected to destroy the score rather than release it.

He lived the last two decades of his life in peace and quiet at Ainola, both a national hero and highly respected internationally. He died – from a cerebral haemorrhage – on 20 September 1957, aged 91.

Rovaniemi is the capital of Lapland. In the depths of winter, temperatures as low as -50 degrees Celsius are not uncommon. Santa's 'head office' is in Rovaniemi and his 'home' is right in the heart of the capital. It's a vibrant holiday destination where you can see reindeer, ride on skidoos over frozen rivers, enjoy some reindeer stew high in the mountains overlooking incredible landscapes, or to go slay riding either by horse or dogs!

Just north of Rovaniemi is the Arctic Circle and, in high summer, everything north of this line is bathed in perpetual daylight for around 70 days which is why Lapland is often called 'the land of the midnight sun'. In mid-winter, the sun doesn't rise at all for about the same period.

Jean Sibelius celebrated his 50th birthday by conducting his *Symphony no. 5 in E flat major* for the first time. It was during World War 1 and later, for a short time, the family left Finland because of the dangers associated with the Russian Revolution.

Sibelius travelled through much of Europe and Great Britain, frequently as a guest conductor. He met with a number of other great composers — Dvořák, Richard Strauss, Mahler and Debussy. He was well respected and, like Edvard Grieg in Norway, received much acclaim during his lifetime.

THESE PAGES: Snow and ice are a part of the Lap landscape for a lot of the year, but it doesn't deter the locals (TOP LEFT) from taking a swim. The snowmen stand guard at Santa's 'Head Office' near Rovaniemi.

Jean Sibelius' last published work was written in 1926. Then he effectively retired. In 1935, on the occasion of his 70th birthday, he made his last public appearance when 7000 guests, including three former presidents of Finland, attended a concert in his honour.

He lived to be 91. Some of his doctors would have been surprised to hear this, but, as Jean said, "All of the doctors who told me not to smoke, or drink alcohol, have died a long time ago. But I'm still living".

In early September 1957, he walked out into the woods and looked up to see a wedge of cranes flying south. He said, "Here they come! The birds of my youth!"

On the 20th of that month he died of a cerebral haemorrhage at 'Ainola'. At the very same time, Malcolm Sargent was conducting Sibelius' fifth symphony in the University Assembly Hall in Helsinki. At his funeral service at the Great Cathedral in Helsinki, 17,000 people paid their last respects. After the death of her beloved Jean, Aino Sibelius stayed on at 'Ainola' until her death in June 1969 — another twelve years.

Most of Sibelius' work — in many ways like Grieg's — was based on the legends and myths of his country. Likewise, much of his rhythm and melody is akin to Finnish folk music. He wrote seven symphonies and started work on an eighth which was never finished and of which there is no remaining evidence. Some say he burned it during the 1940s, others that it never existed. Perhaps we will never know. There is one piece, however, which stands out in most people's minds when the name Sibelius is mentioned — the evocative and enduring *Finlandia*.

For most people, when you mention classical music, it is usually thought of in the past tense — a period in history no longer relevant to present

Helsinki's Cathedral (Tuomiokirkko) is in the city's Senate Square and is one of the most recognised buildings in Finland. The exterior features five green cupolas and white Corinithian columns. Inside are statues of Luther, Melanchthon and Agricola.

times. It may come as a surprise to learn that classical music is alive and well and living in Finland.

Einojuhani Rautavaara studied composition at the Sibelius Academy. A graduate of Helsinki University, he continued his music studies in Vienna, New York and Cologne. He has held numerous posts including Professor of Composition at the Sibelius Academy for 14 years. His list of prizes, memberships and honours is too long to mention, as is his list of works. These include eight symphonies, concertos, chamber music, choral works and folk song arrangements.

In Finland, Einojuhani Rautavaara is a living legend. When he was in his early twenties, Sibelius turned 90. As part of the celebrations Sibelius was granted funding by the Finnish government for a sponsored study tour at the Julliard Institute of Music in New York. Sibelius was asked to select a young Finnish composer of rising note to take up the prize and he selected Einojuhani.

On his return from New York, Einojuhani visited Jean several times at 'Ainola' and they became friends. The 'master' was a great influence on the young Rautavaara. So much so that when Sibelius died, he was one of the chosen pall bearers at his funeral in the Great Cathedral in Helsinki.

Russia

St Petersburg

...St Petersburg was the
centre of high culture in Imperial
Russia. This is where the teenage Tchaikovsky
studied, at the age of twenty-three in 1863, he
decided to take his interest in music seriously
and commence formal lessons at the newly-
founded Conservatory. He was classical
music's most famous, and certainly most
successful, late beginner...

SIMON CALLOW

A city of canals, it's not surprising that St Petersburg is also known as the 'Venice of the North'. Undoubtedly one of the most beautiful cities in the world, St Petersburg is the cultural treasure trove of Russia. In its relatively short history, it has produced a wealth of theatre, ballet and opera companies, singers, dancers, writers and orchestras. Composers Rimsky–Korsakov, Borodin, Mussorgsky, Glinka and, of course, Tchaikovsky are just some of the great names in classical music that the city has given the world.

St Petersburg was the capital of Russia from the early 1700s until 1918. Situated at the head of the Gulf of Finland on the River Neva, even now it's known to many Russians as the 'Northern Capital'. After the revolution of 1914 it was renamed Petrograd then, in 1924, the name was changed again, this time to Leningrad after the famed communist leader. In 1991, following the collapse of communism throughout eastern Europe, the city reverted to its original name.

Throughout history the people of St Petersburg have exhibited exceptional resilience. There have been four floods which wrought massive damage, including in 1824 when the whole city was under water and a total of 462 buildings were destroyed.

One of the greatest stories of heroism and suffering began not long after the German invasion of Russia in 1941. Within ten weeks, the German army had completely encircled the city. So began what Russians call the *Blokada* — the siege of Leningrad. The city had only enough food and fuel supplies to last a couple of months and, by the winter of 1941–42, there was no water, no heating supplies, virtually no electricity and virtually no food stocks. It was an unusually cold winter and during the January and February of 1942 alone, 200,000 people died of cold and starvation.

The siege lasted almost 900 days and, although nobody knows for sure, the estimates of those who died number between 670,000 and 800,000. In 1975 a monument was erected in Victory Square to honour the heroes and survivors of the *Blokada*.

PREVIOUS PAGES: The State Hermitage Museum in St Petersburg – better known simply as 'The Hermitage' – was originally the winter palace of the Tsars and is now the largest art gallery in Russia.
A view over a snowy Senate Square, from the dome of St Isaac's Cathedral.
INSET: Detail of a tiled wall in a disused department store

LEFT: The Summer Palace viewed from across the Neva River.

ABOVE: Horse-drawn sleigh rides provide an atmospheric way to enjoy the extensive grounds of the Pavlovsk Palace in winter.

RIGHT: Panoramic view across the Neva River to the Peter and Paul Cathedral which is contained within the Peter and Paul Fortress. This is where the city of St Petersburg was founded, by Peter the Great, in 1703.

BELOW: Rehearsals about to begin in the Great Philharmonia Hall.

OPPOSITE: Classical Destinations TV series co-presenter, Niki Vasilakis, plays on the stage in the concert hall of the Yusupov Palace. The hall was purpose-built for private concerts for Catherine the Great. It's claimed to be the smallest concert hall in Russia. On a darker note, the palace is where Rasputin was murdered in 1916.

FOLLOWING PAGES: The grand staircase in The Hermitage.

The siege was a tremendous testament to the defiant spirit of the Russian people. People kept working as best they could and Dmitri Shostakovich wrote his seventh symphony, known as the *Leningrad Symphony*, during this period. On 9 August 1942, almost a year into the siege, it opened at the Great Philharmonia Hall to an audience that was hungry and mostly dressed in rags, some carrying weapons, others wearing gas masks.

The Leningrad Radio Orchestra chose to perform Shostakovich's seventh despite the fact that almost half its musicians had died. An instrument was placed on each empty seat as a silent and poignant memorial. Oboist Ksenia Martus recalls, "The music inspired us and brought us back to life; this day was our feast."

The 25-year reign of Josef Stalin from 1929 saw another period of darkness engulf St

Petersburg, and the arts in Russia in general. Stalin used art and culture as another means of propaganda to support the Communist party. His reign of terror left many so-called 'enemies of the state' either killed or exiled to Siberia, and was stifling for the arts. Literature, architecture, painting, dance and music were all heavily censored. Unless it served the purposes of the party, it was considered self-serving or debauched.

However, St Petersburg and its rich heritage of culture somehow managed to survive and the world is the richer for it. There is one person who is largely responsible for how St Petersburg looks today and it's not a man. Catherine the Great was born in the Prussian Kingdom — now part of Germany — in 1729. In 1745 she was married to the heir of the Russian throne who became Peter III.

Catherine was a progressive thinker and a lover of the arts, but it seems she wasn't all that crazy about her husband. In 1762, she engineered a coup against him. He was later killed in an 'accident' and Catherine became the ruler of Russia. Under Catherine, science, the arts and trade flourished. New buildings were added relating to the sciences and fine arts. The first public library was constructed and many educational institutions were established.

The Baroque Winter Palace was originally built for Empress Elizabeth, daughter of Peter the Great and, in 1762, it became the main residence of the Tsars. It's also one of the major attractions in St Petersburg as it is the main building of the world-famous Hermitage Museum. There are 1786 doors, 1945 windows and 1057 halls and rooms, many of which are open to the public. The museum was founded in 1764 when Catherine the Great bought a collection of 255 paintings from Berlin. Today the Hermitage has over 2.7 million exhibits, encompassing an enormously broad spectrum from Ancient Egypt to early 20th century Europe.

THESE PAGES: The Hermitage boasts a lavishly-decorated interior with a total of 1057 halls and rooms (and 1786 doors!). Among the many thousands of artworks are a number by Leonardo da Vinci (OPPOSITE BELOW) as well as Michelangelo, Titian and Raphael.

The collection is so huge it has been calculated that if only one minute was spent in front of each exhibit, it would take 11 years to see everything.

The Hall of St George, also known as the 'Big Throne Hall', is one of the many rooms in the Hermitage and had no purpose other than to demonstrate the wealth and power of Imperial Russia. With people begging for food outside, it's easy to see how a revolution could be enflamed. Yet the irony today is that the Hermitage is a vital part of the life and income of St Petersburg.

The theatre in the Hermitage complex, called Quarenghi's Theatre (after the Italian architect Giacomo Quarenghi who designed the building), was commissioned by Catherine in 1783 and completed in 1787. Performances were given here regularly; sometimes they were only for small intimate groups of friends, sometimes on a grander scale. Catherine loved the theatre, but she didn't like stairs so she had her own private entrance built — off her private living quarters! Quarenghi's Theatre is still used today for exhibitions and concerts.

ABOVE: Quarenghi's Theatre (named after its Italian architect) in the Hermitage was commissioned by Catherine the Great and was designed with a private entrance from her living quarters.

The Peter and Paul Fortress was the first official building in St Petersburg. Peter the Great of Russia wanted a capital and seaport near the rest of Europe so, in 1703, when he reclaimed the lands along the River Neva from Sweden, he decided to build a garrison on an island in the river as protection from attack. Ironically, the Swedes were defeated even before the fort was completed. For this reason, part of it became a high security political gaol and it has housed the likes of Dostoyevsky, Gorky, Trotsky and Lenin's older brother Alexander.

In the middle of the fortress stands the Peter and Paul Cathedral. At over 122 metres, it's still the highest building in St Petersburg. The weathervane on top is a golden angel holding a cross and this has become a symbol for the city. Although the city was founded by Peter the Great, it wasn't named after him, but rather Peter the Apostle.

The cathedral is the burial place of all the Russian emperors and empresses from Peter the Great himself to Alexander III. It is also a noticeably different design to most of the cathedrals in Russia in that it is more Western European in character than Russian Orthodox. This is perhaps not surprising as Peter the Great was intent on developing Russia's peasant economy to compare with the rest of Europe.

ST. PETERSBURG AT A GLANCE

WEBSITE — http://saint-petersburg.com

COMPOSERS — Pyotr Ilyich Tchaikovsky, Nikolai Rimsky-Korsakov, Modest Musorgsky, Mikhail Glinka, Sergei Prokofiev, Igor Stravinsky, Alexander Borodin, Anton Rubinstein, Mily Alexeyevich Balakirev, Dimitri Shostakovich, Alexander Glazunov, Sergei Rachmaninov, César Cui and Anatol Lyadov.

POPULATION — 4.5 million.

CLIMATE

WINTER — cold with snow, average temperatures range from -15 to -5 degrees Celsius.

SPRING — rainy, but drier from April onward, average daytime temperatures range from 5.0 to 15 degrees Celsius.

SUMMER — warm and sunny with temperature up to 30 degrees Celsius in mid-summer.

AUTUMN — sunny and dry until end of October, rain from November, average temperatures range from -5.0 to 5.0 degrees Celsius.

BEST TIME OF THE YEAR TO VISIT — June to July or February to March.

TOP FIVE TOURIST ATTRACTIONS

HERMITAGE ART MUSEUM — St. Petersburg's most impressive attraction; a three-storey Baroque palace on the banks of the Neva, housing Russia's largest art gallery.

ST. ISAAC'S CATHEDRAL — the church which, with its gilded cupola, can be seen from all over the city.

PETER & PAUL FORTRESS — built by Peter the Great as protection against attack by the Swedish army. Inside the complex is the Peter & Paul Cathedral.

ARTS SQUARE AND THE RUSSIAN MUSEUM — the square was designed by Carlo Rossi and contains many museums, concert halls and theatres. The Russian Museum houses the second largest collection of Russian art.

PAVLOVSK PALACE — located 29 kilometres from the city and surrounded by hundreds of acres of parkland.

TOP TWO COFFEE HOUSES

Aprikot — the interior dates back to 1906. At Nevsky 40.

Sever — serving coffee and confectionary since the Soviet era. At Nevsky 44.

MUST SEE SHOPPING LOCATIONS

Open-air souvenir market near the Church of the Saviour of the Spilled Blood.

COMPOSER'S MUSEUMS/HOMES

Rimsky-Korsakov Apartment-Museum — the composer's rooms with music and memorabilia. At Zagorodny Prospekt 28.

State Museum of Theatre & Music — houses an extensive collection of memorabilia and musical items relating to many Russian

composers including Tchaikovsky. At Pl Ostrovskogo 6. www.theatremuseum.ru/eng

Museum of Music (in the Sheremetev Palace) — collections of musical instruments. Also the venue for lectures and concerts. At Naberezhnaya Fontanki 34. www.theatremuseum.ru/eng

GARDENS/PARKS MUST SEE

SUMMER GARDEN — founded by Peter the Great in 1704 and the location of his first Summer Palace. Located next to the Field of Mars and St. Michael's Castle.

CATHERINE GARDEN — a public garden in front of the Alexandriinsky Theatre, designed in the 1820s by Carlo Rossi.

ANNUAL MUSICAL EVENTS

September — Early Music Festivals, www.earlymusic.ru

January — Art's Square Music Festivals, www.artsquarewinterfest.ru

March — Ballet Festivals, www.mariinsky.ru

May to July — White Nights Music Festivals, www.philharmonia.spb.ru

INFORMATION

Tourist Office, Nevsky Prospekt 41, telephone +7 (812) 311 2841, www.spb.ru/eng.

Tour information — www.lenarttours.com

St Petersburg is so full of history, it's hard to believe that it is only 300 years old. The first living quarters built in the newly founded city was a wooden cabin for Tsar Peter himself. Though it was only small, Peter lived there for five years and some of his original belongings still fill the place with a sense of his presence. Peter wanted all the houses in his new city to be built of stone — like the rest of Europe — but he couldn't afford a stone house at the time so he ordered that the walls be painted to look like there were made of bricks.

Almost everything about the way Peter built the city was grand, and the palaces and boulevards were made to be viewed from a distance.

Long before Peter the Great — in 1240, in fact — a Russian by the name of Alexandr of Novgorod is supposed to have defeated the Swedes — on the site where the Alexandr Nevsky Monastery now stands — so earning himself the title 'Nevsky', meaning "of the Neva River". Actually, the battle took place about 20 kilometres away, but the first church here was founded by Peter in 1710 in honour of Alexandr's victory. Peter held the monastery in the highest regard as it trained priests of high rank for the Russian Orthodox Church. The current monastery, designed by Italian Domenico Trezzini, was consecrated in 1724.

OPPOSITE: *The spire of the Peter and Paul Cathedral. All Russia's royalty from Peter the Great to Alexander III are buried here.*

LEFT: The Tikhvin Cemetery is attached to the Alexander Nevsky Monastery and contains the graves of many of Russia's great composers including Tchaikovsky and Alexander Borodin (BELOW). Rimsky-Korsakov, Glinka and Mussorgsky are also buried here.

A walled walkway leads to two very special cemeteries which, together, are called the Necropolis of Masters of Arts. On one side is a gathering of St Petersburg's famous architects as well as the father of Russian science, Mikhail Lomonosov. On the other side are some of the greats of literature and music, including Fedor Dostoyevsky and Peter Tchaikovsky. Another grave here belongs to a composer who is less well known outside Russia, but whose influence on those who followed was huge.

Mikhail Ivanovich Glinka was born in 1804 in Smolensk. Unlike his more famous colleagues in other parts of Europe, for much of his life Glinka was something of an amateur and his compositions remained unsophisticated. Nevertheless his first opera — *A Life for the Tsar*, written in 1836 — established him as Russia's leading

composer. His knowledge of rural folk music and use of nationalistic themes gained Glinka recognition as the founder of Russian nationalism in music. He was also the first Russian composer to be recognised outside his own country and his influence extended to Rimsky-Korsakov, Borodin, Mussorgsky and Tchaikovsky who all acknowledged their debt to him. In fact, Tchaikovsky's first compositions have been said to have borrowed heavily from Glinka.

A little under 30 kilometres south of St Petersburg is the Grand Palace of Pavlovsk which was built for Tsar Paul I and used as his summer residence. The palace is surrounded by hundreds of acres of parklands and dense birch forest given to Paul in 1777 by his mother, Catherine the Great. In 1838 the first Russian railway was built, connecting St Petersburg and Pavlovsk, and it ran into a section

ABOVE: The Pavlovsk Palace, around 30 kilometres south of St Petersburg, is surrounded by hundreds of acres of parkland and birch forest.

RIGHT: The Grand Palace at Pavlovsk was designed by the Scottish architect Charles Cameron and built in the style of an Italian villa. It was completed in 1786 and given to Tsar Paul I by his mother, Catherine the Great. Russia's first railway linked Pavlovsk with St Petersburg in 1838.

of the park called the Great Star. In order to attract St Petersburg society, great dinner parties and concerts were regularly held at the Music Station. These became quite famous after Johann Strauss II started coming as guest conductor in 1856 for a series of performances which became an annual event. Strauss brought the charm of Vienna's music into St Petersburg's cultural life and helped to integrate Russia into the cultural life of the west. Sunday afternoon concerts are still popular here.

Strauss was every bit as popular in St Petersburg as he was in Vienna. In fact, he not only became the idol of Russian aristocrats, but also of their wives. More than once he found himself in difficulty, trying to escape jealous husbands and young girls he'd fancied. Once, it was only by hiding in his consul's coach that he managed to escape an already announced wedding party!

PYOTR ILYICH TCHAIKOVSKY AT A GLANCE

Arguably the most popular of the Russian classical composers by virtue of works such as the explosive (literally) *1812 Overture* and the ballets *Swan Lake, Nutcracker* and *The Sleeping Beauty*, Tchaikovsky was also one of the most innovative and expressive. For a while, his 'popular' output overshadowed his true creative genius in the eyes of music historians and saw him greatly undervalued as composer worthy of a place alongside Mozart or Beethoven.

Pyotr Ilych Tchaikovsky was born on 7 May 1840 in Kamsko-Votkinsk during the reign of Tsar Nicholas I. He was a highly sensitive, even slightly neurotic, child who showed musical abilities from a very early age and who was devastated by the death of his French-born mother when he was 14. Most sources now agree that Tchaikovsky was troubled throughout his life by his homosexuality which, one biography notes, he "endured".

In 1852, the family moved to St Petersburg. His piano teacher advised against a career in music so, at 19, Peter became a government clerk, but continued music studies and playing the piano. When the St Petersburg Conservatoire was opened 1862, Tchaikovsky went there to study and came to the attention of the institution's founder, Anton Rubinstein, who recognised some emerging talent. Tchaikovsky began full-time music studies and, in 1865, was invited to take up the post of Professor of Harmony at the newly-established Moscow Conservatoire. The next year he wrote his first symphony which

wasn't well received at St Petersburg, but earned Tchaikovsky a meeting with Mily Balakirev and 'The Five' group of nationalistic composers which included Borodin and Rimsky-Korsakov. Tchaikovsky always remained apart from the group, but was helped with various projects by Balakirev including the *Romeo and Juliet* overture. His second and third symphonies, an opera, two string quartets and the *Piano Concerto No.1* occupied Tchaikovsky during the first half of the 1870s, then came a disastrous marriage (in 1877) which lasted just ten weeks and pushed the composer to attempt suicide. After a period of recovery in Switzerland, Tchaikovsky returned to Moscow to pursue an even more unusual relationship with a wealthy widow called Nadezhda von Meck. She had earlier employed him on a minor commission, but from this developed a 13-year relationship based solely on intense and intimate correspondence. Nadezhda also supported Tchaikovsky financially, enabling him to concentrate entirely on composing which resulted in a string of significant works including *Swan Lake*, the operas *Eugene Onegin* and *The Maid of Orleans*, the *Symphony No.4 in F minor*, *1812 Overture, Serenade for Strings* and his violin concerto. Another burst of creativity which included the Symphony No. 5 in E minor, The Sleeping Beauty and The Nutcracker, and the opera The Queen of Spades. Tchaikovsky's sixth and most important symphony, the Pathétique, was written just before his death, most likely from cholera, in November 1893.

BELOW: *The Rose Pavilion in the Pavlovsk Palace complex was built as a concert hall and Johann Strauss II conducted here during the 1850s. Today it's again the venue for concerts.*

OPPOSITE: *The dramatic statue of Peter the Great in St Petersburg's Senate Square. Built on the orders of Catherine the Great and known as 'The Bronze Horseman', it's a popular place for just-married St Petersburg couples to stop for wedding photographs.*

In the end, Strauss handed his baton over to Mikhail Glinka to continue the tradition and concerts were held for more than a hundred years. Sadly, the pavilion was destroyed during World War II, but the annual performance was revived at the turn of this century.

Russia's first conservatory of music was opened in St Petersburg in 1862, under the direction of pianist, composer and conductor Anton Rubinstein. In 1871 Nikolai Rimsky-Korsakov joined the staff as a professor and remained for 20 years, but before that he had attended the Naval Academy in St Petersburg. In fact, he wrote his first symphony while on a three-year naval tour of duty.

In 1861 he met the composer Mily Balakirev and, through him, joined the young composers César Cui, Modest Mussorgsky and Alexander Borodin. They later became known as 'The Five' or 'The Mighty Handful'. Partly because of the influence of Glinka, the group stressed their national heritage through their music.

When he joined the St Petersburg Conservatory, Nikolai realised that he knew almost no music theory, although by this time he had composed two symphonies and numerous other works . So he taught himself in secret and became one of the world's greatest music theorists, particularly in music harmony.

Several of Rimsky-Korsakov's students achieved musical greatness, including Sergei Prokofiev and Igor Stravinsky, and his influence was quite profound. He also completed the unfinished works of his friends, Borodin and Mussorgsky. In 1944, on the centenary of his birth, the conservatory was renamed the Rimsky-Korsakov St Petersburg State Conservatory in his honour.

Friend and fellow member of 'The Five', Alexander Borodin is one of the more fascinating Russian composers. His *Prince Igor* is widely acknowledged as one of the greatest Russian operas, but he once said that for him "...music was a pastime — a relaxation from more serious occupations". Born the illegitimate son of an Armenian prince and one of his mistresses, Borodin was probably the most musically gifted of 'The Five' (composing a piano polka when aged only nine), but entered the Medico-Surgical Academy in St Petersburg.

In 1862 he became a professor at the Academy and played a leading role in establishing medical courses for women. He spent most of his life touring, lecturing and supervising student work. However, his home life was chaotic. It seems Borodin and his wife — Ekaterina, a brilliant pianist — lived surrounded by stray cats who were allowed to do as they pleased. Rimsky-Korsakov once complained that when he'd tried to shoo a cat away from his dinner, Ekaterina took the cat's side against him.

OPPOSITE TOP: The sitting room in the apartment where Nikolai Rimsky-Korsakov lived and worked in St Petersburg and which, today, is a museum dedicated to the composer.

OPPOSITE BELOW: Rimsky-Korsakov's piano and portrait on display in the Museum of Music which is housed in the Sheremetev Palace.

NIKOLAI RIMSKY-KORSAKOV AT A GLANCE

During the latter half the 19th century in Russia, an important group of classical composers emerged who were committed to writing music which expressed a national identity. The impetus for this came from Mikhail Glinka (1804–1857) and was further developed by Balakirev, Cui, Mussorgsky, Borodin and Rimsky-Korsakov... this five later became known as the 'Mighty Handful' or, simply, 'The Five'.

Nikolai Andreevich Rimsky-Korsakov was born on 18 March 1844 in Tikhvin near Novgorod. The family was musical and it was discovered early on that young Nikolai had perfect pitch, but his interests lay elsewhere and, at the age of 12, he was enrolled in the Naval College at St Petersburg with the intention of becoming a sailor. While there he saw Glinka's nationalistic operas *A Life for the Tsar* and *Ruslan and Lyudmilla* and then, through his music teacher, met Mily Balakirev who encouraged Nikolai to compose a symphony. This subsequently became his *Symphony No. 1 in E flat* (heralded by César Cui as the first Russian symphony, although, in truth, it was one of the first), but before it was finished Rimsky-Korsakov spent three years in the Russian Navy, still uncertain about a career in music. However, when the first symphony was successfully premiered by Balakirev in 1865, he began to take composing more seriously (although he remained in the navy). At the age of 27 he was offered the position of Professor of Composition at the St Petersburg Conservatoire and, two years later, also became the Inspector of Military Bands. Both jobs enabled him to closely study orchestration, his natural talents in this area subsequently enhanced by his greater understanding of technique. This became evident in subsequent orchestral works such as *Scheherazade*, *Capriccio Espagnol* and *Russian Easter Festival Overture*; all intensely colourful and characterful compositions.

After the death of his close friend Mussorgsky, Rimsky-Korsakov orchestrated the opera *Boris Godunov*, although earlier versions exist with music by its original composer. Rimsky wrote 15 operas of his own, including *Sadko*, *Christmas Eve*, *Mozart and Salieri* (based on the rumour that Mozart was poisoned by his rival), *The Tsar's Bride* and *Servilia*.

His teaching position at the Conservatoire, combined with the popularity of his music (not to mention its nationalistic themes), made Rimsky-Korsakov a very influential figure in Russian music at the start of the 20th century.

By now, of course, Russia was in a state of upheaval and Rimsky-Korsakov's last opera, *The Golden Cockerel* (which made fun of the Tsarist authorities) was banned. In fact, it was never seen by its composer who died on 21 June 1908, but whose considerable influence continued for many decades afterwards through his illustrious students who, in addition to Glazunov, included Sergei Prokofiev and Igor Stravinsky.

The Church of The Saviour on the Spilled Blood

is built on the site where Tsar Alexander was

assasinated while helping a small boy.

It was during his work on Borodin's *Prince Igor* that Rimsky-Korsakov wrote some of his own most colourful work — the *Spanish Prince* and *Sheherazade*.

Undoubtedly Russia's best known classical composer is Pyotr (Peter) Illyich Tchaikovsky. He studied at the St Petersburg Conservatory for three and a half years. However, his graduation piece — a cantata — wasn't considered very good by the conservatory's director, Anton Rubinstein. In spite of this, after he graduated, Peter was immediately given a post at the newly-established Moscow Conservatory, as professor of harmony. The director was Anton Rubinstein's brother, Nicholas, whose house Tchaikovsky shared for five years.

In 1874, when Tchaikovsky finished his first piano concerto, he took it to Anton Rubinstein whose criticism was that it was "derivative, trite and vulgar". He urged many changes, but Tchaikovsky refused. Instead he dedicated the concerto to the German pianist Hans von Bülow who was so flattered that he chose to premiere the work in Boston, during a US tour, on 25 October 1875.

The story for many of Tchaikovsky works was one of the experts rejecting them, but the people loving them. However, after a while, Anton Rubinstein did change his mind about the first piano concerto and, as both a pianist and a conductor, performed it often.

Tchaikovsky's music was well received outside Russia and he was one of the few composers who gained wide acceptance during his lifetime. His work as a music critic for the *Russian News* took him to Bayreuth in Germany for the first full performance of Wagner's epic *The Ring*. Tchaikovsky's comments to his brother Modeste were that "…as music it is unbelievable chaos, through which there flash from time to time remarkably beautiful and striking details. It may be a great masterpiece, but there surely is not anything more boring or long-winded than this interminable thing". He later conceded that *The Ring* was "…one of the most significant events in the history of art".

Tchaikovsky travelled extensively and, unlike his contemporaries — Rimsky-Korsakov, Borodin and others of the Russian nationalist movement — was greatly influenced by the music of the west. He met a number of composers including Liszt and Wagner and, in Paris, got to know Saint-Saëns. He also heard Bizet's *Carmen* there, an event, he said, which changed his life. The combination of music and drama captured his imagination and inspired him.

In 1877, Tchaikovsky married one of his pupils from the Moscow Conservatory, Antonina Milyukova. After only nine weeks he threw

PREVIOUS PAGES: The ornate Church of the Resurrection of Jesus Christ, also known as the Church of the Saviour on the Spilled Blood… as it marks the place were Alexander II was fatally wounded by an assassin on 1 March 1881, while apparently helping a small boy. The centre picture shows the souvenir market in front of the church.

ABOVE: Inside the courtyards of the Winter Palace. From the 1760s, this was the main residence of the Tsars and its oppulence — not to mention the extravagant lifestyles of Russia's rulers while the general populace struggled — undoubtedly helped sow the seeds of revolution.

OPPOSITE TOP: The Alexander Nevsky Monastery was designed by the Italian architect Domenico Trezzini and completed in 1724. The site is symbolically important as it's where a Swedish fort once stood during the Northern War between Russia and Sweden.

himself into an icy river in order to get pneumonia and die. A secretive, highly emotional and unhappy homosexual, Tchaikovsky tried to solve his desperate situation with a socially acceptable marriage. His brother Modeste brought him back to St Petersburg where he suffered a complete nervous breakdown. Ironically, this period saw the creation of some of his greatest work notably the opera *Eugene Onegin* — based on a story in verse by Pushkin — the *Violin Concerto in D*, and the *Symphony No.4 in F minor.*

At about this time, a wealthy widow called Madame Nadezhda von Meck approached Tchaikovsky about writing a piece for her. He said he would not write for money, but then turned around and asked for her financial support to help him finish writing a symphony. He also sent her a photograph of himself. She did send him some money and continued to do so for the next 13 years. It was an unusual relationship in that Madame von Meck insisted that they never meet. "The more fascinating you are to me," she wrote, "the more afraid I am of making our acquaintance."

It was the perfect arrangement for the shy composer. When they once met face-to-face at a concert, they turned from each other in embarrassment and not a word was spoken.

BELOW: One of Tchaikovsky's pianos is part of the extensive collection of important historical instruments held in the Museum of Music.

The Mariinsky Opera and Ballet Theatre dates back to 1859 and was severely damaged during the Siege of Leningrad. Its stage, seen here with the fire curtain lowered, has been graced by many of the great names in opera and ballet including Vatslav Nizhinsky, Anna Pavlova and Rudolf Nureyev.

For a period Tchaikovsky conducted the orchestra at the Mariinsky Theatre, and his *Symphony No.5 in E minor*, as well as the fantasy overture *Hamlet*, had their premieres there. In 1869 Marius Petipa became the chief choreographer at the Mariinsky. Petipa produced Tchaikovsky's ballets *Sleeping Beauty* and *Swan Lake*, although the latter was not a success until Petipa rechoreographed it after the composer's death. Tchaikovsky was the first composer Petipa had allowed into his creative process and it is said that their collaboration brought ballet out of the realm of light entertainment and into the world of dramatic, expressive art. The distinctive green-and-white Mariinsky Theatre was named in honour of Tsar Alexander II's wife, Maria. It was built in 1859 as an opera house, but its reputation rests on ballet, especially as it's home to the most famous of ballet companies, now the Mariinsky, but known during the Soviet era as the Kirov.

In 1891 Tchaikovsky visited the USA where he conducted the orchestra at the gala opening of Carnegie Hall in New York. He said himself that he was more famous in America than in Europe and it was probably true.

Tchaikovsky's final symphonic work is considered to be his most important. The *Symphony No.6 in B minor* is also called the *Pathétique* (a name suggested by his brother Modeste after 'Tragic' was discounted), but within a week of its premiere in St Petersburg on 28 October 1893, Tchaikovsky was dead. It's said that he carelessly drank a glass of unboiled water, knowing that cholera had been rampant in the city, and died of the disease within a couple of days. The troubled life of Pyotr Illyich Tchaikovsky was over, but his music lives on. In fact, in opera houses and concert halls around the world, he is probably the most played of the late 19th century composers.

BELOW: Arts Square. Even in spring St Petersburg is still snowy and cold.

Arts Square is a perfect example of the extensive planning which went into the making of St Petersburg. It was designed by Italian-born Carlo Rossi who spent most of his working life in Russia. In fact, most of his contemporaries — and even present day art historians — call him by his Russian name of Karl Ivanovich Rossi. Rossi built the most important building in the square, the Mikhailovsky Palace which today houses the Russian Museum, home to the second largest collection of art in the country. Also in Arts Square is the Ethnography Museum which represents all the ethnic cultures of the former USSR, and the Great Concert Hall, or *Bolshoi Zal*, of St Petersburg Philharmonia — the city's prime venue for classical music concerts.

Another notable building is the Mussorgsky Theatre which was built

in 1833 and originally known as the Maly Opera and Ballet Theatre. From the middle of the 19th century to the early 20th century, its stage saw a number of great performances of German, French and Italian operas by foreign companies. Following the Russian Revolution in 1917, it became home to more Russian artists and has always been the theatre which staged all the new ballets and operas by Shostakovich, Prokofiev and Stravinsky.

Modest Mussorgsky, like many of the early Russian composers, also had a 'real' job to begin with. Mussorgsky was born in 1839 and, like compatriot composer Borodin, he was musically gifted as a child — first performing to an audience when aged nine. At the age of 13 he entered the Guards' Cadet School in St Petersburg and pursued a career in the army while continuing to compose. In 1857 he met and studied with Balakirev and became one of 'The Five', resigning from the army in 1859. Mussorgsky was a heavy drinker — a habit he acquired at Cadet School. He

ABOVE: The statue of Alexander Pushkin in Arts Square. The building behind is the Russian Museum, one of the many museums, theatres and concert halls which surround the square.

OPPOSITE: St Isaac's Cathedral dominates the skyline of St Petersburg. It took 40 years to build and was finished in 1858. It can accommodate a congregation of up to 14,000 people.

started and abandoned two operas, but in 1868 he began work on *Boris Godunov* which was eventually accepted by the Imperial Theatre. On its premiere in 1874, it was a great success with audiences, but musicians found its unconventional methods and unusual style difficult.

Mussorgsky's heavy drinking sapped his ability for concentrated work. The last few years of his life were creatively very patchy, although one of his best known compositions, *Pictures at an Exhibition*, was written at this time. In 1881, he suffered an alcoholic seizure in the street and was taken to hospital where he died a month later — a week after his 42nd birthday.

MODEST MUSSORGSKY AT A GLANCE

An erratic life shortened by alcoholism – which also resulted in a much smaller output than that of his compatriots – initially meant Mussorgsky's considerable talents often went largely unrecognised by music historians. Over time, however, he has come to be acknowledged as one of the greatest Russian composers and certainly an important member of the 'Mighty Handful' (or *kouchka* in Russian) alongside Rimsky-Korsakov, Cui, Balakirev and Borodin. This informal group of composers all worked in the latter half of the 19th century and were united in their search for a uniquely Russian style of music.

Modest Petrovich Mussorgsky was born in Karevo on 21 March 1839 and, like Rimsky-Korsakov, showed early musical ability, but was more interested in pursuing a military career. He gave his first concert performance, playing a Field piano concerto, when aged 11 by which time the family had moved to St Petersburg. At 13 he went to the Imperial Guard's military academy and, four years later, joined the Preobrajensky Regiment where, it's said, he first learned to drink heavily. When 19 Mussorgsky met the highly influential Mily Balakirev and became his first pupil. As with Rimsky a few years later, Balakirev convinced the young Mussorgsky to begin composing, although the earliest works have disappeared. In 1858, he resigned from the army to concentrate on his music and went to Moscow where he began to gain a wider appreciation of his Russian heritage. Returning to St Petersburg, Mussorgsky continued to receive tuition from Balakirev, but it appears he produced little of real consequence from this period.

In 1861, Tsar Alexander I liberated the serfs, forcing Modest and his brother Philaret to take over the running of the family estate. Neither was capable of the task and, within a couple of years, the Mussorgsky family was destitute. Modest took a job as a government clerk and returned to composing albeit again without any notable success. In 1865, he suffered his first alcoholism-related collapse and went to live with his brother in order to recover. This low point in Mussorgsky's life also marks a turnaround because he now began to show some of the genius for which he is recognised today, first with a series of songs, including *The Nursery* cycle, and then with his masterful opera, *Boris Godunov*. Based on the Pushkin play, *Godunov* was initially rejected by the Imperial Opera who thought it too unconventional. By now sharing a flat with Nikolai Rimsky-Korsakov, Mussorgsky reworked the opera which was resubmitted in 1872... only to be rejected again. However, a year later, three scenes were staged by the Imperial Opera for a benefit concert and the performance was a great success. The rights were acquired by a music publisher and the entire opera performed in early 1874 to considerable audience acclaim, but a lukewarm response from the critics (including, incidentally, Balakirev and Cui). Nevertheless, the work continued to be performed (and, it has to be said, revised) and today is considered the greatest Russian opera. Also premiered in 1874 was *Pictures at an Exhibition*, a musical tribute to the artist Viktor Hartmann and originally written for the piano, but later orchestrated by Ravel. *Pictures* demonstrates Mussorgsky's brilliant interpretative skills and emotional intensity. Who knows what might have eventuated had he not died, shortly after his 42nd birthday, from alcoholism-related paralysis.

The gilded dome of St Isaac's Cathedral is a landmark that can be seen from all over St Petersburg. Completed in 1858, it took 40 years to build and was one of the greatest architectural constructions of the period. Over 100 metres high and almost as wide, it can hold up to 14,000 people.

An imposing monument to Nicholas I dominates the centre of St Isaac's Square. The first houses were built here in the 1760s and the oldest building is the Myatlev's mansion where the renowned poet Alexander Pushkin would visit his friend and fellow poet Ivan Myatlev. In the 1840s the Ministry of State Property was begun, as was the beautiful Mariinsky Palace, a wedding gift from Nicholas I to his daughter, the Great Duchess Maria. Nowadays, the building houses the St Petersburg legislative assembly.

In St Peterburg's main square — called the Palace Square — there are some great examples of how different architectural styles can be combined to dramatic effect. On the northern side of the square is the magnificent baroque Winter Palace, built in 1762. In the opposite direction, on the southern side, is the classical yellow-and-white building of the former Imperial Army General Staff, built by Carlo Rossi between 1819 and 1829. The Triumphal Arch, also a classical design, leads through to Nevsky Prospekt, the main boulevard of St Petersburg. To the west, the square borders The Admiralty with its gardens. In the centre is the Alexander Column, built to commemorate Russia's victory over Napoleon and nearly 48 metres in height. The column itself is a single piece of red granite weighing over 600 tonnes — an amazing feat to hoist up in 1834! Incidentally the angel's face is said to have been modelled on that of Tsar Alexander I.

The Hotel Astoria was built in 1912 and has been the hotel of choice for visiting artists and dignitaries. The guest list from over the years is impressive — Maxim Gorky, Fedor Shalyapin, Isadora Duncan, Anna Pavlova, members of the Royal Romanov and Fabergé families. The Astoria's Presidential Suite is where many of the world's visiting foreign heads of State stay when in St Petersburg.

In the hotel's Winter Garden Hitler bragged he would celebrate with a dinner when he took the city. Thanks to the spirit of the Russian people, it never happened, but the room is still there. Indeed, the fact that St Petersburg's rich heritage can be enjoyed today is a testament to the city's remarkable — and inspirational — capacity for survival.

BELOW: Panoramic view of St Isaac's Square in early spring with the Hotel Astoria seen at the centre of the photograph.

Puccini Verdi

Italy

Tuscany

...Just before Liu's demise,
the tenor is given Puccini's greatest
hit — Nessun dorma, or 'None shall sleep'.
Contrary to modern practice, it sounds better
from one tenor than three, even if its
sense of victory makes it a natural
for football tournaments...

SIMON CALLOW

*T*uscany is certainly one of Italy's best-known regions and its distinctive landscapes — invariably bathed in warm and inviting sunlight — have become synonymous with romance and 'getting away from it all'. Vineyards, olive groves, hill-top villages, rustic farmhouses and the evocative slender cypress trees undoubtedly helped promote Tuscany as a rural retreat, but in reality the northern part — between Florence and Lucca — is both densely populated and highly industrialised. The region's economic importance dates back to the Middle Ages, but it's also renowned for hugely significant contributions to both the arts and sciences. In addition to Florence and Lucca, all Tuscany's key towns and cities — among them Pisa, Siena, Arezzo, Prato and Elba — are steeped in history, dating back, of course, to the Romans.

Lucca, for example, was established in 180 BC. It was part of the
Roman province of Cisalpine Gaul and governed by Julius Caesar. It is
one of the few Roman towns in Italy that still has its ancient walls,
although the original fortifications were built over with more substantial
ramparts during medieval times and again during the 16th and 17th
centuries. Today these wide walls are a public park and provide extensive
views of the city.

Lucca's church of San Giovanni e Reparata was built in the 5th
century, but its place in classical music history was assured on 23
December 1858 when a one-day-old baby was christened Giacomo
Antonio Domenico Michele Secondo Maria. The surname? Puccini.

Young Giacomo represented the fifth generation of a musical family
who had mostly been involved with Lucca's Duomo San Martino
(cathedral) as organists and choirmasters. He was the fifth of seven
children and the 15th century house where he was born — now known as
Casa di Puccini — is a museum, containing manuscripts, portraits,
costumes and, perhaps most interestingly, the piano on which he
composed his last opera, *Turandot*.

Giacomo was just five when his father died and he subsequently
inherited the position of church organist and director of music at the
cathedral. The job was actually done by his uncle until Puccini was
sufficiently well trained to take over. However, the young musician's life
changed dramatically in 1876 after he saw a performance of Verdi's
towering opera *Aïda* in Pisa. Legend has it that he walked the 20
kilometres from Lucca to Pisa because he only had sufficient funds for the
opera ticket. It was, however, worth the effort because Puccini
subsequently committed his life to opera… and opera alone.

After completing his musical studies at Lucca's Conservatorio Pacini, Puccini went to Milan where the Teatro alla Scala (La Scala Theatre) was very much the home of Italian opera. In 1880 he entered the Conservatorio Reale where he was taught by the composer Amilcare Pochielli, whose only surviving work is the opera, *La Giaconda*.

Just prior to graduating in 1883, Puccini took part in a competition for one-act operas and created a work called *Le Villi* in co-operation with his librettist, Ferdinando Fontana. He was unsuccessful in the competition, but after playing excerpts from the opera at a party attended by many influential people in the music world, he attracted the attention of the influential Milanese publisher Giulio Ricordi. Ricordi acquired the rights to *Le Villi* which was subsequently expanded to two acts and staged, to great acclaim, in Milan's Teatro dal Verme in 1884. This led to the commissioning of a new opera which, in contrast, failed badly and was later described by Puccini as "a blunder". Nevertheless, his relationship with Ricordi survived and, indeed, lasted a lifetime. The publishing house was subsequently rewarded with *Manon Lescaut*, first performed in Turin in 1893 and considered by many to be Puccini's most masterful opera. It was certainly appreciated by the audience at the premiere

OPPOSITE AND BELOW: The famous 'Leaning Tower' of Pisa – the Campanile alongside the city's cathedral in the Campo dei Miracoli (the Field of Miracles) — was built on sandy subsoil and started to tilt as the third storey was completed. Prior to recent work to reduce the lean, the tower was 5.4 metres out of vertical.

Puccini

GIACOMO PUCCINI AT A GLANCE

The last of the great Italian composers from the Romantic era, Giacomo Puccini was born on 22 December 1858 in the Tuscan town of Lucca, near Pisa. The family had a long history in church music as both organists and composers at Lucca's Duomo San Martino, and Giacomo was expected to continue the tradition. However, in 1876 he attended a performance of Verdi's great opera *Aïda* and was so moved by the experience that he committed his life to this musical form.

In 1880, after studying music at the Conservatorio Pacini in Lucca, he went to Milan and continued his education at Conservatorio Reale where his graduating work was an orchestral piece called *Capriccio sinfonico*. It was a great success and illustrated Puccini's gift for both inventive melodies and lively orchestration.

His first opera, the one-act *Le Villi*, was initially written for a competition in which it was unsuccessful, but when Puccini subsequently performed some excerpts from it at a party, he received great acclaim. As a result *Le Villi* was subsequently staged in May 1884 in Milan and attracted the attention of the music publisher Giulio Ricordi who acquired the rights and commissioned a new opera. It wasn't a success, but Puccini's next work, *Manon Lescaut* most definitely was and, after its premiere in Turin in 1893, his fame quickly spread through Italy and beyond.

His reputation was further enhanced by his next three operas – *La Bohème* (1896), *Tosca* (1900) and *Madama Butterfly* (1904) – which have endured as his most popular and oft-performed works. Incidentally, when it was first performed in Turin in 1896, *La Bohème* failed to impress the critics, although today it is considered by many to be Puccini's finest opera. Likewise, the first performance of *Madama Butterfly*, at Milan's La Scala Theatre, was a disaster, but after the opera was revised and relaunched in 1906 it, too, became a huge success.

Also in 1904, Puccini was finally able to marry his lover (and mother of his only child), Elvira Gemignani, who was the wife of a Lucchese merchant. Their relationship commenced in 1886, but despite her long-term infidelity, Elvira maintained some Catholic sensibilities and wouldn't contemplate marriage to Puccini until her first husband died. Elvira later caused another scandal after, ironically, she accused a housemaid of having an affair with Puccini and subsequently hounded the girl to her death (by suicide) which resulted in legal proceedings. Keen to put this tragedy behind him, Puccini looked for a greater operatic challenge which came with *La Fanciulla del West* set in the Californian gold rush in the mid-1800s and featuring Wild West tunes. It premiered in New York in 1910.

After a brief falling out with his publisher, Ricordi, Puccini wrote *La Rondine* (The Swallow) for a Viennese theatre director and it was first staged in Monte Carlo in 1917. The Austrian connection got him into trouble at home as, in WWI, Italy fought on the side of the Allies. It didn't help matters when he suggested German occupation might improve Paris.

Puccini's last opera, the masterful *Turandot*, is also considered his greatest, although the last act was yet to be finished when he died in Brussels on 19 November 1924, of throat cancer.

who demanded over 30 curtain calls. It also guaranteed Puccini's fame and led George Bernard Shaw, then a music critic, to herald him as the true heir to the great Giuseppe Verdi.

While still working on *Manon*, Puccini purchased a house beside a lake in the village of Torre del Lago which has subsequently been renamed to reflect its long association with the composer. Torre del Lago Puccini is connected by a beautiful avenue of lime trees — the Via dei Tigli — to the Italian seaside town of Viareggio. With its grand hotels and villas, Viareggio was one of Europe's first seaside resorts and, particularly during the latter half of the 19th century, was frequented by both artists and aristocracy.

Puccini chose his lakeside retreat at Torre del Lago primarily because of his passion for duck shooting, but it undoubtedly also provided him the peace and seclusion for composing. He became a close friend of the owner of the Lago di Massaciúccoli and its surrounding territory, the Marchese Carlo Ginori-Lisci. In fact, he dedicated his next great opera, *La Bohème*, to the Marchese.

In *La Bohème*, one of the four main characters, Mimì, dies in the final scene after being reunited with her lover Rodolfo. Puccini wrote this scene late one night and, upon finishing it, later recalled, "I had to get up and, standing in the middle of the study, alone in the silence of the night, I wept like a child. It was like seeing my own child die".

However, he then apparently joined friends for a night of excessive drinking. By all accounts Puccini liked a party and enjoyed many drinking sessions at an inn in Torre del Lago which was later renamed the Café alla Bohème.

BELOW: Behind these old stone walls is a typical Tuscan villa surrounded by vineyards and, later in the year, fields of sunflowers.

Scenes from around the Lago di Massaciúccoli, the lake on which Giacomo Puccini liked to hunt waterfowl. He purchased a villa nearby in the village of Torre del Lago (BELOW) which has since adopted his name.

WEBSITE – www.luccaturismo.it

COMPOSERS – Giacomo Puccini, Nicolò Paganini.

POPULATION – 81,870.

CLIMATE

WINTER – cold, but temperatures rarely drop below zero degrees Celsius.

SPRING – mild with average daily temperatures ranging from 8 to 18 degrees Celsius.

SUMMER – hot with daily temperatures often rising to 35 to 38 degrees Celsius.

AUTUMN – cool and frequently wet with daily temperatures in the region of two to ten degrees Celsius.

BEST TIME OF THE YEAR TO VISIT – Spring or during the month of September when a series of religious events are held for the Volto Santo (Saint Face) festival.

TOP FIVE TOURIST ATTRACTIONS

LE MURA (City Walls) – ramparts built between 1500 and 1645, now a public park.

ANFITEATRO ROMANO (ancient Roman Amphitheatre) – only a few original stones remain in Lucca's Piazza del Mercato.

DUOMO DI SAN MARTINO – 11th century cathedral with many artworks include a painting by Tintoretto.

S. MICHELE IN FORO – Pisan-Romanesque church, famous for its elaborate façade.

TORE DEI GUINIGI (Guinigi Tower) – on Via del Quarquonia, provides stunning views of the city and the Apuan Alps.

TOP TWO COFFEE HOUSES

L'Antico Caffè delle Mura, Piazza Vittorio Emanuele II, 1.

Caffè di Simo, Via Fillungo.

MUST SEE SHOPPING LOCATIONS

VIA FILLUNGO – Lucca's principal shopping street with many bars and cafes along the way.

COMPOSERS MUSEUMS/HOMES

CASA NATALE DI PUCCINI (Puccini's birthplace) – on Corte San Lorenzo 9. 15th century house where Puccini was born in 1858, contains the piano on which the opera Turandot was composed.

MUSEO VILLA PUCCINI – on Piazzale Belvedere Puccini. Puccini's lakeside home in Torre del Lago purchased in 1891and now a museum. Both the composer and his wife, Elvira, are buried here.

GARDENS/PARKS MUST SEE

PARCO FLUVIALE (River Park) – parklands on the banks of the Serchio River near the town centre, forms an 11 kilometre circuit for walking and bike riding. Many picnic sites along the river.

ORTO BOTANICO (Botanical Gardens) – Via del Giardino Botanico 14.

PALAZZO PFANNER – Via degli Asili 33, formal gardens with a central avenue lined with numerous Baroque statues.

ANNUAL MUSICAL EVENTS

April to July – Sagra Musicale Lucchese, Lucca Sacred Music Festival with concerts held in various churches.

July – Summer Festival, blues and rock music, www.summer-festival.com

July to August - Festival Puccini at Torre del Lago Puccini, www.puccinifestival.it

September to October - Del Giglio Theatre, www.teatrodelgiglio.it

INFORMATION

APT Lucca, Piazza Santa Maria 35, telephone +39 (0)583 919931, email info@luccaturismo.it

Now undoubtedly Puccini's most popular opera, *La Bohème* received a cool reception at its premiere in Turin in February 1896, and critics compared it unfavourably with *Manon Lescaut*. However, its lighter style and more realistic dialogue have guaranteed its continued acceptance by modern audiences.

Puccini's personal life could certainly have been the basis for an opera. When still a young man he began a long relationship with a married woman, Elvira Gemignani, which in 1886 led to the birth of a son, Antonio. However, with divorce forbidden in Catholic Italy, the couple had to wait until the death of Elvira's husband in 1904 before they could be united.

However, Elvira was distrustful of her new husband — there was apparently some substance to her concerns — which eventually led to a tragic incident. After finding Giacomo chatting to the couple's young

ABOVE: Classic Destinations *TV series co-presenter Matt Wills following in the footsteps of Puccini on the road from Lucca to Pisa. In 1876, when aged 18, the composer walked the entire distance to attend a performance of Verdi's opera Aïda.* The experience moved him sufficiently to dedicate his life to opera.

LEFT: Puccini's piano in his villa at Torre del Lago Puccini, which is now a museum

OPPOSITE BELOW: The city of Lucca was originally founded as Roman colony in 180 BC. Its ramparts, built in the 16th and 17th century, have since been converted into tree-lined walkways which offer expansive views over terracotta-tiled roofs.

Today the strains of Puccini's works can be heard across the Lago di Massaciúccoli from the open-air opera theatre built after his death and dedicated to the composer. It's the venue for the annual Festival Puccini held in July and August.

housemaid late one night, Elvira accused the girl of being her husband's mistress and began pursuing her relentlessly. This went on for weeks and eventually the young girl, whose name was Doria Manfredi, eventually locked herself away and committed suicide by drinking poison. The subsequent autopsy revealed she was still a virgin. Doria's brother demanded revenge and prosecuted Elvira for menace and defamation. Puccini wanted to settle out of court, but Elvira went through with the trial and was found guilty, fined and sentenced to a prison term of five months and five days. Upon appeal, Puccini was finally able to settle on an amount of 12,000 lire which allowed the Manfredis to erect a monument to Doria and buy a cottage for themselves by the lake. Not surprisingly, this incident nearly separated the couple and it was only towards the end of the composer's life that the relationship was restored.

Professionally, though, Puccini went from success to success, and his fame spread far beyond Italy. In 1910, *La Fanciulla del West* — which is set in a Californian gold mining camp — had its debut in New York with Caruso in the leading role and conducted by Toscanini. Another New York debut took place in 1918 with *Il Trittico*, but his opera *La Rondine* (The Swallow) which had its debut in Monte Carlo a year earlier was considered Germanic enough to warrant questions about his patriotism — Italy fought with the Allies in WW1. Matters weren't helped when he was reported to have implied that Paris would be improved by the German invasion of the city. For a time, all his operas were banned in Italy.

GIUSEPPE VERDI AT A GLANCE

Considered Italy's greatest composer, Giuseppe Verdi was born on 10 October 1813 in the village of Le Roncole near Busseto in the Italian region of Emilia-Romagna. He was the son of an inn-keeper and, like so many before and after him, began to show musical ability while still very young. When he was ten, his father sent Giuseppe to Busseto for musical tuition which was paid for by a local merchant, Antonio Barezzi. Young Verdi rewarded his patron by quickly developing his compositional talents and, when aged 19, he was sent to Milan with the intention of joining the Conservatorio. However, he was refused admission – the reasons vary from being to old to lacking the necessary academic aptitude – so Verdi instead took private lessons from Vincenzo Lavigna who was a conductor at Milan's famous Teatro alla Scala (La Scala Theatre).

After two years of tuition in Milan, Verdi returned to Busseto in 1836, but again the intended plan – to take up the organist's position at the cathedral – didn't eventuate. His patron, Barezzi, secured Verdi a directorship with the Philharmonic Society at a modest salary, and the young composer began working on his first opera, *Oberto, Conte di Bonifacio*. He also married his benefactor's daughter, Margherita. When *Oberto* was accepted for production at La Scala, the couple – now with two small children, Icilio and Virginia – moved to Milan. *Oberto* was a great success but Verdi suffered a triple tragedy when both his children died within days of each other followed by Margherita about three months later. Grief-stricken and struggling with the failure of his second opera, Verdi was ready to abandon both music and Milan, but he was persuaded to attempt a third opera by the impresario Merelli who showed him a libretto on the life of the Old Testament king Nebuchadnezzar. The resulting opera, *Nabucco*, was staged at La Scala in 1842 and was a triumph, bringing Verdi both fame and fortune. His future assured, Verdi began writing operas in quick succession, sometimes up to two a year, and his themes of a free and united Italy saw him identified with the *Risorgimento*.

In 1847 Verdi met the soprano Giuseppina Strepponi and the two lived together for 12 years before finally marrying. Stability in his private life fostered stimulation in his professional life, and Verdi's three most popular operas – *Rigoletto, Il Trovatore* and *La Traviata* – were all written within the period 1851 to 1853. After the first free Italian parliament was instituted in 1860, Verdi was elected to the legislative assembly and remained in politics for five years. Returning to composing, Verdi's subsequent operas included *Don Carlos*, the spectacular *Aïda* (written to celebrate the opening of Cairo's opera house), *Otello* and his final great work, *Falstaff* which premiered in Milan in 1893. Although by then nearly 80, Falstaff was as energetic, imaginative and expressive as any of Verdi's earlier operas. After suffering a stroke, Giuseppe Verdi died in Milan on 27 January 1901.

Puccini's last opera, *Turandot*, was commenced in 1921 by which time the composer had moved from Torre del Lego to Viareggio to be closer to treatment for a growing number of ailments. He was eventually diagnosed with throat cancer and died on 29 November 1924, in Brussels while undergoing treatment, at the age of 65. *Turandot* was unfinished, and the last two scenes were completed from his notes by the composer Franco Alfano. At the opera's debut in Milan's La Scala in April 1925 (again conducted by Toscanini), it was left in the unfinished form, but on the second night it was performed with Alfano's closing scenes. Both Puccini and Elvira are buried in a mausoleum at the home in Torre del Lago, now the Museo del Puccini.

Giacomo Puccini can be said to have helped 'modernise' opera, bringing it into the 20th century in a fashion that was more accessible to audiences and, in some ways, laying the foundations for the modern musical. He understood the need for dramatic storylines which would absorb audiences and he wrapped these in haunting melodies and rich orchestrations which added to the intensity of the whole experience. The young man whose life was changed by Verdi's *Aïda*, subsequently became known as "the most important Italian opera composer since Verdi".

Giuseppe Verdi was born in 1813 in the village of La Roncole, near Busseto in the region of Emilia-Romagna which is south of Tuscany.

Verdi displayed musical aptitude from an early age and, when just ten, he was sent to Busseto for tuition from the local church organist. Giuseppe came from a poor family, but obtained sponsorship from Antonio Barezzi who was a wealthy businessman and music lover.

Barezzi even took the young Verdi into his home and employed him in his grocery business.

With further financial support from Barezzi, Verdi was sent to Milan to study at the Conservatorio, but at 19 he was considered too old and was refused admission. Instead he undertook private studies with Vincenzo Lavigna who was a conductor at La Scala. After two years in Milan he returned to Busseto to take up the position of church organist following the death of his old teacher. However, a reputation for wild living saw the post go to a rival, but Verdi ended up as *maestro di musica* for the Philharmonic Society which pleased him equally. Furthermore he married Antonio Barezzi's daughter Margherita and began work on his first opera, *Rocester*, which has subsequently been lost, but it's thought some of the music was incorporated into his next work, *Oberto, Conte di San Bonifacio*. This was accepted for production at La Scala so, in 1839, Verdi — now with a young family — returned to Milan. *Oberto* premiered at La Scala on 17 November 1839 and was an immediate success, bringing a commission for three further operas from the theatre's manager. However, within a tragically short period, both Verdi's young children died, followed by Margherita. His grief was compounded by the failure of his next opera,

The small town of Busseto – not far from Parma on the road between Bologna and Milan – is where a young Giuseppe Verdi went for tuition. He was subsequently sponsored, employed and housed by a local merchant who probably didn't realise just where his patronage would lead.

COMPOSERS MUSEUMS /HOMES

Barezzi House and Hall

Orlandi Palace

Giuseppe Verdi's birthplace at Roncole Verdi (Casa Natale di Giuseppe Verdi), telephone +39 (0)524 97450.

Villa Verdi at Sant'Agata – Verdi's farm, purchased in 1849 and located just north of Busseto.

Verdi Theatre – built in 1857.

ANNUAL MUSICAL EVENTS

Winter opera season and summer opera season (open air theatre)

July – opera singing contest

INFORMATION

Tourist Office telephone +39 (0)524 92487, fax +39 (0)524 931749, email info@bussetolive.it

WEBSITE – www.comune.busseto.pr.it

COMPOSERS – Giuseppe Verdi (born in Le Roncole, Bussetto in 1813).

POPULATION – 6840.

CLIMATE

Winter – cold with average daily temperatures from -1 to +4 degrees Celsius.

Spring – mild-to-warm with daily temperatures from 9 to 18 degrees Celsius

Summer – hot and dry with daily temperatures in mid-summer often exceeding 30 degrees Celsius.

Autumn – mild and often foggy in late autumn with average daily temperatures from 10 to 16 degrees Celsius.

Best time of the year to visit – Spring (March to May) and autumn (September to November).

TOP FIVE TOURIST ATTRACTIONS

Civic Museum in Villa Pallavicino.

Monte di Pietà Palace (dates back to 1679).

Giovanni Guareschi's birthplace (author of the Don Camillo stories).

Church of San Bartolomeo.

Church of SS Trinità.

TOP TWO COFFEE HOUSES

Pasticceria Muggia – founded in 1867.

Salsamenteria Baratta – the perfect venue for gourmet music-lovers.

Un Giorno di Regno and, close to nervous collapse, Verdi tried to withdraw from all operatic commitments. He was talked out of it by La Scala's manager, the impresario Merelli, and began work on *Nabucco*, based on the story of the Old Testament king Nebuchadnezzar. This opera's full title is actually *Nabucodonosor*, but the abbreviated name is used today.

Premiered at La Scala, *Nabucco* marked a change in fortunes for Verdi… in fact, it was a triumph. His personal life also took a turn for the better and Verdi began living with Giuseppina Strepponi, the young soprano who had been instrumental in helping bring *Oberto* to the stage. The couple lived, unmarried, at the Palazzo Orlandi in Busseto, apparently much to the consternation of the locals.

Nabucco's theme of national independence struck a chord with the audiences of the day as many of Italy's duchies or states were under Austrian rule (including Tuscany). *Nabucco* is credited with inspiring the *Risorgimento* (resurgence) which was a movement dedicated to liberating and reunifying Italy. It took five decades of struggle, but after Venice and then Rome fell to royalist troops, in 1870 Italy finally became a unified kingdom.

Verdi's contribution extended beyond his nationalist operas and, from 1861 to 1865, he was a member of the national parliament which was established when much of Italy was freed from Austrian rule (and Turin was the capital).

After living with her for 12 years, in 1859 Verdi eventually married Giuseppina who, by all

Thanks to the generosity of Antonio Barezzi in fostering Verdi's career, Busseto now has a very important place in the history of Italian opera.

accounts, was a very positive force in the composer's life. Certainly some of his most successful operas, at least in terms of popularity, were written after the pair became a couple — *Rigoletto*, *Il Trovatore* and *La Traviata*. They lived in a farm at Sant'Agata near Busseto, but also travelled extensively including many visits to Paris and one to St Petersburg where he composed a work for the Imperial Theatre. The grand opera which so inspired Puccini, *Aïda*, was written in 1871 to celebrate the opening of the Italian Theatre in Cairo (and not, as is sometimes claimed, the opening of the Suez Canal). Verdi's

final two operas are generally acknowledged to be his best — *Otello* based on Shakespeare's play Othello, and *Falstaff* which was also sourced from the Shakespearean character in *The Merry Wives of Windsor* and *Henry IV*. *Falstaff* was written in 1893 when Verdi was 80. Giuseppina died of pneumonia in 1897 and while the great love of his life could never be replaced, Verdi found some solace in a relationship with the singer Teresa Stolz who was 20 years his junior, but whom he'd known for many years previously.

Towards the close of 19th century, Giuseppe Verdi's health deteriorated markedly but he lingered on until January 1901 when, during a visit to Milan, he suffered a stroke. He died on 27 January, aged 87, and it's estimated 200,000 people lined the streets as his body was carried to the oratory in the Musician's Home that Verdi himself had helped establish. Acknowledged as Italy's greatest composer, the peasant who became a patriot wrote over 40 operas during his long lifetime and, while some influences were evident early on, Verdi is distinguished by his originality and inventiveness which helped inspire a revolution... and continues to inspire audiences

Unlike many of the classical composers, Verdi enjoyed comparatively early success and was able to buy a farm near the village Sant'Agata, north of Busseto, which is now the Villa Verdi museum.

Venice

*...It is hard not to be
pierced by the beauty of Venice,
which always seems to me — in the right
light — to have emerged from the sea, rather
than to be sinking into it... the very place
seems to have been turned into music
by the composers of the Italian Baroque
—Vivaldi and Monteverdi...*

SIMON CALLOW

The city of canals, Venice is also synonymous with music and romance. Located on the northeast coast of Italy at the northern end of the Adriatic Sea, Venice is built on more than 100 islands in a swampy lagoon in the Gulf of Venice. It was first established as a settlement nearly 1600 years ago and became an independent Byzantine province in the 10th century. Trading links with the east brought immense wealth and, with this, patronage of the arts. During the 12th, 13th and 14th centuries Venice was a world power and its influence remained strong until it was conquered by Napoleon 1797.

Austrian rule was established in 1815 and it wasn't until 1886 that Venice became part of the newly reunited Italy.

The oldest bridge in Venice is the Ponte di Rialto which was built in the late 1500s and is one of the city's most famous sights. For hundreds of years it was the only way to cross the Grand Canal – Venice's main waterway — into one of the city's oldest quarters.

Built on a swamp, many of the construction techniques used in Venice are unique and involved impermeable stone supported by rafts and timber piles. Testimony to the success of these techniques is that a great many buildings are over 400 years.

Once described as the most beautiful street in the world, the Grand Canal is lined with palaces, or *palazzi*, built over a period of five centuries and once owned by Venice's greatest families. The Palazzo Barbarigo still has the remnants of 16th century frescoes on its façade. The Palazzo Farsetti and Palazzo Loredan were built around 1200 and now house the Venice City Council. In 1807, Napoleon watched a regatta held in his honour from the Palazzo Balbi which today houses regional government offices.

After passing the Rialto the canal doubles back along a stretch known as La Volta (the bend). The Ponte dell'Accademia was the second bridge built over the canal, although not until 1854, and is named after the Accademia which houses the world's greatest collection of Venetian paintings.

At the end of the Grand Canal is the church of Santa Maria della Salute, built to commemorate the end of the plague which ravaged the city in 1630 — the word "salute" means health and salvation. This magnificent Baroque church took 57 years to construct and its immense weight is supported by over a million timber piles.

PREVIOUS PAGES: Dusk over one of Venice's famous canals — the light trails have been created by a passing power boat. INSET: Statues of angels adorning the central arch of the Basilica di San Marco, Venice's best-known church.

OPPOSITE: A gondola on The Grand Canal which is Venice's 'main highway' and winds through the centre of the city. It's lined with many palazzi, built between the 13th and 18th centuries.

ABOVE: Sunrise over the Piazza San Marco.

Venice's best-known church is undoubtedly the Basilica di San Marco (in the Piazza San Marco) which features five huge domes and is the third building to stand on this site. The first dates back to the 9th century and enshrined the body of St Mark. It was destroyed by fire in 976 and the second church was then deliberately demolished to make way for a grander construction that better reflected Venice's growing status. The altar at the back of the basilica supposedly houses the remains of the saint which were thought to have been lost in the fire, but mysteriously reappeared when the new building was consecrated in 1094.

A Mass was held at the Basilica di San Marco in 'thanksgiving for deliverance' from the plague, and its composer was Claudio Monteverdi who was the church's choirmaster, or *maestro di capella*.

Born in Cremona, northern Italy, in 1567, Monteverdi is said to define the transition from the

ABOVE: The Baroque church of Santa Maria della Salute is supported by over one million timber piles, and was built to celebrate the city's deliverance from the plague of 1630.

OPPOSITE TOP: Gondolas have been a part of the Venetian scenery since the 11th century and are ideally suited to the narrow canals.

OPPOSITE BELOW: People compete with pigeons for space in front of the Basilica di San Marco.

Renaissance style to the Baroque. His first published work — a book of sacred songs — appeared in 1582 when Monteverdi was aged 15. In 1590 he moved to Mantua to become a poorly-paid musician in the court of the Duke of Mantua, but later was appointed the *maestro di capella* at the town's cathedral. He wrote his first opera, *L'Orfeo*, in 1607 which was the same year his wife, Claudia, died. This event plunged the composer into a deep depression which lasted several years and he returned to Cremona. A second opera, *Arianna*, was written in 1608 to celebrate a court wedding and was a huge success. He was appointed to the Basilica di San Marco in 1613 where he finally began to receive a good salary and his musical emphasis shifted towards sacred works, including the great Mass. However, Monteverdi, who became a priest in 1632, also wrote secular music and, when Venice's first opera house opened in 1637, he was invited to contribute to the repertoire. Initially, *Arianna* was revived, but then he wrote two new operas plus a ballet for the court at Piecenza. Monteverdi's final opera was *L'Incoronazione di Poppaea* written in 1642 when he was 75. The original is now held in Venice's Biblioteca Marciana which is also in the Piazza San Marco. Monteverdi died in Venice in November 1643 and is buried in the church of Santa Maria Gloriosa dei Frari.

...the bright clarity of what they wrote directly

translates the space and the clear light of the square

in front of the Basilica of San Marco into sound.

ANTONIO VIVALDI AT A GLANCE

One of the most recognised pieces of classical music is *Le Quattro Staggioni — The Four Seasons*; four violin concertos written by Vivaldi and first published in 1725. Today it is one of the most performed and recorded classical works ever, beloved for its depiction of seasonal change through music evocative of spring's awakening, an approaching summer storm or winter's icy stillness. *The Four Seasons* is also considered quintessentially Italian in its light and shade which, in truth, is more of a statement about Vivaldi's capabilities as a composer of concerti which are full of vibrancy and vigour.

Antonio Lucio Vivaldi was born in Venice on 4 March 1678. Little is known of his childhood, but his father was a violinist at the Basilica di San Marco and is likely to have been Antonio's first music teacher. At 15 he commenced training for the priesthood, finally taking Holy Orders ten years later in 1703. There's some question marks over his application to the calling which may have been health related (it's thought Vivaldi suffered from asthma) or may have been related to the distraction of priorities which lay in the direction of music.

After his ordination, Vivaldi was appointed music teacher to the Ospedale della Pietà, an orphanage for girls attached to the church of the Pietà (the Santa Maria della Visitazione). He remained associated with the orphanage for virtually his entire life, but it needs to be understood that the Venetian *ospedali* ran an extensive program of musical events which included many public concerts for which Vivaldi composed choral works and sacred music. He was also required to write Masses and other liturgical pieces.

Some time around 1712, Vivaldi began writing his first opera and is thought to have subsequently written over 100, although only around half has survived. In 1716, he was appointed *maestro dei concerti* at La Pietà and, between 1718 and 1721, was also music director to the court at Mantua under Prince Philip of Hesse-Darmstadt. It was during this time that he met the singer Anna Giraud (known as 'La Girò') who caused considerable consternation by becoming his constant travelling companion... what's more, along with her sister!

However, his musical fame, continually bolstered by his prodigious output, easily overwhelmed any scandal and, in 1728, Vivaldi enjoyed several audiences with Emperor Charles VI. He subsequently dedicated two collections of music, *La Cetra* (Op. 9), to the emperor.

In 1737, perhaps as a result of his relationship with Anna, Vivaldi was banned from staging his operas in the papal territory of Ferrara and, in 1739, his contract at La Pietà wasn't renewed. The following year he left Venice for Vienna, probably with a view to working for the Imperial Court, but the War of Austrian Succession intervened and Vivaldi was left unemployed. He died on 28 July 1741, penniless, and was buried in a pauper's grave. Vivaldi left behind over 800 works (the exact number is still unknown), the majority undated, but remarkable for their scope, diversity and depth of expression.

Thirty-five years later Venice gave birth to another important Baroque-era Italian composer. Antonio Lucio Vivaldi was the first son of a barber-turned-violinist at San Marco who trained the boy on the instrument.

ABOVE: The baptismal font in the Gothic church of San Giovanni in Bragora where, in 1678, Antonio Vivaldi was christened.

OPPOSITE TOP: Unwanted babies were deposited through this chute at the Ospedale della Pietà, an orphanage for girls that was attached to the Chiesa Santa Maria della Pietà. Vivaldi, who was also a priest, taught music at the orphanage.

RIGHT: The Metropole Hotel is built on the site of the original orphanage on the Riva degli Schiavoni.

He showed early musical aptitude, but coming from a comparatively poor family, he was compelled to join the priesthood in order to obtain an education. Antonio was ordained in 1703, but shortly after ceased saying Mass, claiming a chest condition — thought likely to asthma — which often forced him to stop mid-service and leave the altar. Some biographers have suggested this was merely a ruse so that he could quickly write some musical idea while it was still fresh in his mind. Apparently, Vivaldi didn't suffer any shortness of breath when playing the violin or conducting an orchestra! It appears safe to conclude that Vivaldi was more dedicated to music than the church, although he was diligent in many 'good works'. Most notable of these was the musical training of orphaned girls who were taken in by the Ospedale della Pietà. Attached to the church of La Pietà, Santa Maria della Visitazione, unwanted new-borns were deposited in a chute to be collected and cared for by the orphanage.

The church of the Pietà specialised in the musical training of girls and it was rumoured this education was so good that well-off families would

RIGHT AND BELOW: Today the church of the Pietà is known as 'La Chiesa di Vivaldi', or 'The Church of Vivaldi'. When participating in services, the girls from the orphanage were kept hidden behind laced ironwork.

also leave their babies to be brought up and trained at the Pietà. This prompted the Pope to have a sign placed on the orphanage which read, "May the Lord God strike with curses and excommunications all those who send, or permit their sons and daughters — whether illegitimate or natural — to be sent to this hospital of the Pietà, having the means and ability to bring them up. For they will be obliged to pay back every expense and amount spent on them. Neither may they be absolved unless they make atonement, as is clearly set out in the bull of our Lord Pope Paul III, November 12, 1548".

In 1703, Antonio Vivaldi was appointed *maestro di violino* at the orphanage and, over the next

VENICE AT A GLANCE

WEBSITE – www.turismovenezia.it

COMPOSERS – Claudio Monteverdi, Alessandro Scarlatti, Antonio Vivaldi, Richard Wagner.

POPULATION – 269,560.

CLIMATE

WINTER – cold with average temperatures between 0 and 7 degrees Celsius.

SPRING – frequent rainfall with average temperatures between 7 to 17 degrees Celsius.

SUMMER – hot and humid with daily temperatures reaching 28 to 30 degrees Celsius in mid-summer.

AUTUMN – frequent heavy rainfall with possible flooding, average temperatures range from 9 to 18 degrees Celsius.

BEST TIME OF THE YEAR TO VISIT – Attractions all year round, but can be extremely crowded during the summer months (July to September).

TOP FIVE TOURIST ATTRACTIONS

THE SIGHTS OF PIAZZA SAN MARCO (St Mark's Square) – Palazzo Ducale (the Doge's Palace), Museo Correr (the Correr Museum), the Bridge of Sighs, the Campanile, Basilica di San Marco (St Mark's church), Museo ARCHEOLOGICO (Museum of Archaeology).

PONTE DI RIALTO (the Rialto Bridge) – famous stone bridge which crosses the Grand Canal.

TORRE DELL'OROLOGIO (the Clock Tower) – elaborate clock in the Piazza San Marco built-in the 15th century with clockwork figurines and enamelled face.

CA' REZZONICO (the museum of 18th century Venice) – a palazzo housing frescoes, furnishings and paintings from the

18th century and once owned by the poet Robert Browning.

ACCADEMIA – a superlative collection of paintings of the Venetian school, dating from the Byzantine period.

TOP TWO COFFEE HOUSES

Caffé Florian – San Marco.

Gran Caffé Quadri – San Marco.

MUST SEE SHOPPING LOCATIONS

RIALTO BRIDGE AND RIALTO MARKETS – famous for its street stalls selling food and fresh produce.

PIAZZA SAN MARCO – fashionable shops including shoes, clothing and accessories.

COMPOSERS MUSEUMS/HOMES

Museo della Musica (the Music Museum) –

Campo San Maurizio, San Marco; houses an extensive collection of Baroque musical instruments.

Chiesa di Vivaldi ('Church of Vivaldi') – on the Riva degli Schiavoni, Castello. Vivaldi taught at the orphanage attached to the church.

Palazzo Giustinian – San Marco; Richard Wagner lived here over 1858-59 and wrote the opera Tristan und Isolde.

Palazzo Vendramini Calergi – Renaissance palace on the Grand Canal where Richard Wagner was residing when he died in 1883.

GARDENS/PARKS MUST SEE

Giardinetti Reali – San Marco.

Biennale Gardens – otherwise known as the Giardini di Castello and the site of the Venice Biennale International Art Exhibition, held every odd year. One of the very few public parks in Venice.

ANNUAL MUSICAL EVENTS

Extensive year-around concert and opera programs are held at the following major venues in Venice.

Teatro La Fenice, Campo San Fantin, www.teatrolafenice.it

Teatro Malibran, Campiello Malibran, www.teatrolafenice.it

Ateneo San Basso, San Marco, www.virtuosidivenezia.com

Scuola Grande San Teodoro, Campo San Salvador, Rialto, www.imusiciveneziani.com

INFORMATION

APT Venice, Giardini Reali, San Marco, telephone +39 (0)415 298711, email info@turismovenezia.it

15 years, spent most of his time educating the young ladies of the Pietà. Situated on the Riva degli Schiavoni, the church of La Pietà is now also known as 'La Chiesa di Vivaldi' — the Church of Vivaldi. The ceiling fresco, "Triumph of Faith", was painted by Giambattista Tiepolo in 1755. The church is still popular for its concerts, always with a distinct Vivaldi flavour.

Venice's Metropole Hotel in San Marco is built on the site of the original orphanage where Vivaldi composed and occasionally played until 1740. The interiors are mainly Baroque and, in the kitchen area, remnants of the old building can still be seen.

The hotel is located on the promenade known as the Riva degli Schiavoni which is one of the liveliest parts of Venice. It is always busy and the Venetian water buses — or *vaporetti* — stop here frequently. There are plenty of places to shop for souvenirs and the views across the Canale di San Marco to the island of San Georgio

Giovanni Bellini's Madonna and Child with Saints *which was painted in 1505 and can be seen in the church of San Zaccaria, not far from the Piazza San Marco.*

Maggiore are a reminder of the location's great natural beauty.

Not far off the Via degli Schiavoni is the church of San Zaccaria which was founded in the 9th century, with a Gothic façade which was added in the 15th century. Inside are frescoes and a remarkably lumunous piece of Renaissance art — the *Madonna and Child with Saints* painted by Giovanni Bellini in 1505.

As noted earlier, for many centuries Venice was a powerful, independent republic. This republic was ruled by princes known as Doges. Behind the Basilica di San Marco is the Doge's Palace, or the Palazzo Ducale. It was founded in the 9th century as a castle, but catastrophic fires over the next few hundred years resulted in extensive rebuilding in the 14th and 15th centuries. Sadly most of the artworks of great painters like Fabriano, Bellini and Titian were destroyed by fire in the 1500s, but the architecture — particularly the distinctive pink Veronese marble on the exterior — remains intact.

The Palazzo Ducale includes a torture chamber and the Inquisitor's rooms were linked to the old prison by the Bridge of Sighs. In the 19th century, the English poet Byron invented the name "bridge of sighs", saying it was inspired by the sighs of the prisoners who walked across to their fate at the hands of the Inquisitor. In reality, the Inquisition was well and truly over before the bridge was built. Incidentally, Casanova was imprisoned here, and escaped through a hole made in the Palazzo's roof.

The Hotel Danieli was originally built as the palace of Doge Andrea Dandolo and, hence, is also known as the Palazzo Dandolo. The palace became a hotel in 1822 and was popular with artists and writers. The French composer Claude Debussy stayed here, as did Richard Wagner. Charles Dickens also enjoyed the comforts of the Danieli. One of the most celebrated hotels in Europe, it was built nearly 700 years ago and was the venue for the first court opera to be performed in Venice — Monteverdi's *Proserpina Rapita* in 1630 (unfortunately subsequently lost).

As well as teaching at La Pietà and playing the violin, Vivaldi was composing extensively and his first opera had its debut in 1713. It's thought he subsequently wrote over 100 operas, but over half of them have since been lost. Following his appointment as

BELOW: An early morning view across the Canale di San Marco.

FOLLOWING PAGES: Classical Destinations *TV series co-presenter and concert violinist Niki Vasilakis plays on the Ponte dei Carmini.*

It's easy to get close to Vivaldi in Venice. He lived in quite a number of places which today are guesthouses, hotels and restaurants.

maestro dei concerti at La Pietà, Vivaldi travelled extensively to present his operas. In 1718 he was appointed to the court of Prince Philip of Hesse-Darmstadt who was governor of Mantua. While here Vivaldi met a singer, Anna Giraud (known as La Girò), who became his travelling companion… incidentally, along with her sister. Vivaldi visited Rome and played for the Pope then, a few years later, he had several audiences with Emperor Charles VI. In 1729 he toured Germany and visited the Imperial Court in Vienna. He received a number of commissions from foreign rulers, including Louis XVth of France for whom he wrote *Festival on the Seine*. Despite his extensive travels, Vivaldi remained in the employ of La Pietà, and was required to send them two concertos per month. In 1740 he decided to leave Italy and move to Vienna, in all likelihood to seek employment from his admirer Charles VI. However, it wasn't to be; Charles died in the same year and Vienna was preoccupied with the War of Austrian Succession. Antonio himself died in Vienna on 28 July 1741, aged 60, and was buried in a pauper's grave attached to St Stephen's church.

It's interesting to note that, by this time, Vivaldi had fallen out of favour with the Italian public and, probably due to his relationship with Anna Giraud, his operas were banned in the Papal territory of Ferrara. The directors of La Pietà had also refused to renew his contract.

Perhaps as a result of this fall from favour at the end of his life, after his death, Vivaldi's works virtually disappeared and many weren't rediscovered for close to two centuries. Yet today he is one of Italy's better known classical composers, particularly through the much recorded and performed *The Four Seasons* — four concertos for violin and orchestra which were first published in Amsterdam in 1725. However, up until the early 1900s, Vivaldi's name was largely known only to students of Baroque music who would have undoubtedly been impressed by the Italian composer's clear influence on J.S. Bach… surely a testimony to the former's importance.

A view along the Rio della Pietà, the small canal which runs from nearby the Chiesa di Vivaldi into Venice's Castello region, and was very likely to have been regularly travelled by the composer.

What changed was the discovery, in 1926, of a large hoard of original music scores in a boarding school in the mountains of northern Italy. Hoping to sell the papers to raise funds, the school approached the Turin National Library to have somebody identify and value them. Upon opening the first crate, Dr Alberto Gentili saw Vivaldi's name on the manuscripts and immediately realised the importance of what had been discovered. He also noticed that, from the way they were numbered, that about half the manuscripts were missing. Dr Gentili eventually tracked down the remaining works — they had been part of a split inheritance some 140 years before (and are now known as the Foa and Giodarno collections). In 1939, this enormous body of works was acquired by the Turin National Library, and the world began to rediscover the genius of Antonio Vivaldi. It's thought that some of his prolific output — now numbering over 800 works — still remains to be rediscovered, but regardless, Vivaldi's place in classical music history has already been well and truly assured.

Eisenach
Weimar

…Bach is the pivotal figure in the history of 'classical' music. If there were a physical pantheon of the composers in this book, he'd probably be on the biggest pedestal. No musician is unaffected by him. His melodic inspiration is inexhaustible, the tunes seeming to generate themselves; there seems to be no reason why they would ever come to an end…

SIMON CALLOW

*J*ohann Sebastian Bach has been called 'The Father of Classical Music' and there's little doubting the magnitude of his contribution. He was born in 1685 — the youngest of eight children — in the central German town of Eisenach, but the Bach family's involvement in music was already well established. It was, of course, to be significantly enhanced by Johann Sebastian's generation and the next, so much so that the Bachs have been described as the "grandest of all musical tribes". His father, Johann Ambrosius, was the court trumpeter and manager of Eisenach's town music.

Eisenach, in the state of Thuringia, is also linked with another great name in history — Martin Luther. The Protestant reformer went to school here — the same school later attended by Bach — and took refuge in the town after being declared an outlaw by church and state. It was during this latter period that Luther translated the Greek New Testament into German while residing in Eisenach's 11th century hilltop fortress which is called the Wartburg. This imposing edifice is also said to have been the setting for a scene in Wagner's opera *Tannhäuser*.

With its clean, crisp air Eisenach is known as a summer resort and in many ways it's the quintessential central German town, supporting industries such as spinning, woodworking, cabinet-making, brewing, pottery, alabaster ware and shoe-making. It also offers much to attract lovers of the arts and it's steeped in history, having been established in the mid-12th century. The Nikolaikirche stands next to the town gate which was built in 1180; and around every corner is encountered a peculiar blend of the modern and the gothic.

PREVIOUS PAGES: Classical Destinations TV series co-presenter Niki Vasilakis in front of Berlin's iconic Brandenburg Gate.
The imposing Wartburg fortress looks over the town of Eisenach.
INSET: The Reuter Wagner Museum in Eisenach.

OPPOSITE: Eisenach has many links with classical music, but perhaps the most important is that it was the birthplace of Johann Sebastian Bach.

ABOVE: Martin Luther's room in the Wartburg. After being charged with heresy and threatened with death, Luther was given refuge in the castle by a supporter, the Elector of Saxony.

LEFT: Martin Luther went to school in Eisenach. One hundred and ninety years later, J.S. Bach went to the same school. The composer later became an ardent Lutheran and his faith greatly influenced his music.

The house where Johann Sebastian Bach was born has disappeared over time, but nearby is the Bachhaus which is over 600 years old and now a museum dedicated to his life and music. The Bachhaus collection includes archives and manuscripts as well as an extensive and valuable assortment of old musical instruments.

As if a family of eight children wasn't already big enough, it appears the Bach home was also shared with various relatives and a number of apprentices who were being trained in music by Johann Ambrosius. The youngest Bach was also taught by his father, learning to play the violin and the harpsichord, although it's also recorded that he possessed an exceptional soprano voice, ensuring a place in both church and school choirs.

The Georgenkirche — the Church of St. George — dates back to 1196, although most of what is seen today is from the mid-1500s. In the church is the font at which Johann Sebastian was christened on 23 March 1685. The organist here was his uncle, Johann Christoph Bach, who later taught the boy to play this instrument as well. By all accounts, Johann Sebastian was an enthusiastic and diligent student who soon became an extremely proficient musician. However, his early life was marred by family tragedies — first the death of an elder brother, and then,

a month after his ninth birthday, his mother died. Within less than a year,
his father also died. Johann Sebastian was taken in by his eldest brother,
another Johann Christoph, who lived in the village of Ohrdruf, about 50
kilometres south-east of Eisenach. Johann Christoph was a former pupil of
Pachelbel, and the organist at the Michaeliskirche in Ohrdruf.

A year before this he had been enrolled at the Old Latin Grammar
School in Eisenach where, in addition to Latin, he was taught arithmetic,
history and religion. No doubt his religious studies would have included
the Reformation — very possibly in the same rooms that, 190 years
earlier, Martin Luther had been taught. While this geographical link may
not have made much of an impression on the young Bach, the choirboy
who developed into a church organist and composer could not help but
be influenced by Lutheranism. He became fiercely committed to the
Lutheran Church's doctrines and was described as having an "unshakeable"
faith in God — the inspiration for a prodigious output of religious music
written, above all else, for His glorification.

Martin Luther was born some distance away in Eisleben, but his mother's
family was from Eisenach and he was sent here to finish his schooling. His
mother's relatives were too poor to look after him and so he ended up living
at the school and earning money as a 'kurrende singer' — in other words, as
a busker. A lady called Frau Ursula Cotta took pity on the young Luther and
let him stay in her house which is now a museum in Eisenach's Lutherplatz.
A painting in the house depicts Frau Cotta, but the main attraction is an
exhibition called *Rediscovering Martin Luther* which provides a fascinating look
at the history and culture of Europe in the 15th and 16th centuries with
special emphasis, of course, on the role Luther played.

EISENACH AT A GLANCE

WEBSITE – www.eisenach.de

COMPOSERS – Johann Sebastian Bach, Johann Christoph Bach, Georg Philipp Telemann, Richard Wagner.

POPULATION – 44,100.

CLIMATE

WINTER – average temperatures range from -3.5 to +1.5 degrees Celsius. Moderate to heavy snowfalls in some areas.

SPRING – average temperatures are from 3.0 to 12 degrees Celsius

SUMMER – July and August can be warm and humid with average daily temperatures exceeding 25 degrees Celsius.

AUTUMN – average temperatures range from 5.0 to 14 degrees Celsius.

BEST TIME OF THE YEAR TO VISIT – Spring through to autumn (April to October) provides plenty of attractions for music lovers.

TOP FIVE TOURIST ATTRACTIONS

WARTBURG CASTLE – 11th century fortress overlooking the town and where Martin Luther took refuge in 1521. www.wartburg-eisenach.de

BACHHAUS – museum devoted to the life

and works of J.S. Bach. At Frauenplan 21. www.bachaus.de

LUTHERHAUS – the home where Martin Luther lodged during his school days at Eisenach. At Lutherplatz 8. www.lutherhaus.de

REUTER WAGNER MUSEUM – the most extensive collection of Richard Wagner after Bayreuth. At Reuterweg 2.

GEORGENKIRCHE (Church of St. George) – 12th century church where Luther was a choirboy and Bach was baptised. In Am Markt.

TOP TWO COFFEE HOUSES

Konditorei & Cafè Brüheim, Marienstrasse 1.

Toccata – named, of course, after Bach's Toccata And Fugue in D minor. At Markt 2.

MUST SEE SHOPPING LOCATIONS

Karlsstrasse.

Querstrasse.

COMPOSERS MUSEUMS/HOMES

BACHHAUS – contains an extensive collection of musical instruments as well as J.S. Bach memorabilia. www.bachhaus.de

REUTER WAGNER MUSEUM – the Reuter

Villa (in Helltal Valley) contains over 20,000 items relating the Wagner and opened in 1897.

GARDENS/PARKS MUST SEE

KARTAUSGARTEN – site of a Carthusian monastery which became royal kitchen gardens in 1700 and includes the Wandelhalle – the pump room for a spa that was never built.

ANNUAL MUSICAL EVENTS

March/April – Thuringian Bach Weeks.

May to September - Wartburg Concerts.

September to June - Symphonic Concerts at the Theatre.

All year – Chamber music concerts at the Bachhaus and at the Reuter Wagner Museum.

All year – Church music at Georgenkirche.

INFORMATION

Tourismus Eisenach GmbH, Markt 9, 99817 Eisenach, Germany. Telephone +49 (0)3691 79 230, email info@eisenach.info, www.eisenach.info

Even as a young man, he struggled with what he considered his sinful condition. Nonetheless, when his father wanted him to study law at the University of Erfurt, he yielded and by the age of 21 had earned a Master of Arts degree, enabling him to teach. However, he had lost all interest in law and his studies turned increasingly to religion. When a close friend died, it drew eternity into sharp focus for Martin Luther. Shortly after this, he was caught in open country by a violent thunderstorm and, in his fear, he cried out to St. Anne to save him, promising that if he lived, he would become a monk. He survived the storm and fulfilled his promise to enter the cloister, but inner peace still eluded him. Studying the Bible more closely, he found that the peace he sought was not something he could either earn or buy — it was a free gift. This brought him into direct conflict with the established church which was making a fortune selling people absolution from their sins in the form of 'letters of indulgence' — in other words, tickets to heaven.

Luther's convictions led him to openly question the practice in a document called *The Ninety-five Theses* which, on the eve of All Saints' Day, 31 October 1517, he nailed to the door of Wittenberg's Castle Church, or Schlosskirche, where he was professor of theology. This moment is seen as the beginning of the historical period known as the Reformation. It was important not just because of the birth of the Protestant church, but because it began to encourage wider freedom of thought and expression, effectively paving the way for many of the great composers.

After the posting of his criticisms at Wittenberg, Martin Luther was summoned to what was effectively his trial where the highest ranking officials of both the church and state were present. Nobody could show in the Scriptures where Luther was wrong, but when he refused to recant, he was excommunicated by Pope Leo X and the Emperor, Charles V, made him an outlaw which meant anybody could arrest him. Fortunately, the Prince of Saxony — Elector Frederick the Wise — was a supporter of Luther and arranged to have him kidnapped, taken to Eisenach and placed

ABOVE: A statue of a young J.S. Bach, erected in the centre of Arnstadt. He came here in 1703, when aged 18, to take up the position of organist.

BELOW: Old St John's Cemetery in Leipzig. Bach was originally buried here after his death in 1750… remarkably in an unmarked grave. His remains were exhumed in 1894, identified and reburied inside the Johanneskirche (St John's Church). After this building was destroyed in WW2, Bach's body was moved to the Thomaskirche (St Thomas's Church) in 1949.

JOHANN SEBASTIAN BACH AT A GLANCE

Johann Sebastian was born on 21 March 1685 in the central German town of Eisenach. He was said to possess a fine soprano voice and studied the organ under his brother, Johann Christoph, with whom he lived after being orphaned when aged nine. In 1700, J.S. gained a position as a boy soprano in the choir at Lüneberg's Michaeliskirche. It was here, while still a teenager, that his first compositions were produced. In 1705 he made a pilgrimage — walking 215 miles — to Lübeck to meet the great composer and organist Dietrich Buxtehude who had a significant influence on his music. In 1707, after overstaying his leave from Arnstadt (by three months!), Bach moved to Mühlhausen as organist and married his cousin, Maria Barbara. Fleeing conflict within the Lutheran church (to which he was passionately dedicated), Bach took up an appointment, in 1708, as court organist and chamber musician to Duke Wilhelm Ernst at Weimar. After being passed over for the coveted position of *kapellmeister* at Weimar, Bach moved to the court of Prince Leopold at Köthen... where he was appointed director of music. At Köthen, Bach's output of secular works increased and included violin concertos, chamber music and suites for orchestra. A notable work from this time is the *Brandenburg Concertos*, dedicated to Duke Christian Ludwig of Brandenburg. Maria Barbara died in 1720 — while Bach was away — and 18 months later he married Anna Magdalene, daughter of a town musician. The first

24 preludes and fugues from the "the 48" — which later became known as *The Well-Tempered Klavier* (keyboard) — appeared in 1722, one in each key. The second 24 weren't completed until 20 years later.

Bach's position at Köthen ended with the death of Prince Leopold in 1723, and he subsequently moved to Leipzig to take up the position of cantor at the Thomasschule... a post he would hold until his death. Now Bach's output became even more prolific — both sacred and secular works, including five complete cycles of cantatas for the church year (he wrote a total of 295 church cantatas). The oratorio *St John Passion* was performed for the first time 1724 and the *St Matthew Passion* in 1729, the same year Bach became director of the Collegium Musicum in Leipzig. Bach's Lutheran faith was the overwhelming influence on his music during the latter half of his life and, while Handel's *Messiah* may be better known, Bach's four 'Passion' settings (including the *Easter Oratorio* and the *Christmas Oratorio*) are considered to be equally if not more devout.

In 1749 Bach's sight began to fail, but he managed to finally finish his *Mass in B minor* which had been begun in 1724. An operation to correct his eyesight — performed by the same surgeon who operated on Handel — wasn't successful, but ironically Bach's sight mysteriously returned just ten days before he died. The classical composer who vies with Mozart for the title of "the greatest" died, as the result of a stroke, on 28 July 1750.

in protective custody in the Wartburg. Here he lived for the better part of a year, growing a beard and assuming the name of Junker Jörg.

Luther called this period his "wilderness", but it was also one of his most productive. In addition to translating the New Testament from Greek to German, he wrote a number of essays on topical issues and a collection of Christmas sermons which he personally considered his best work.

In 1999 the castle of the Wartburg was placed on the World Cultural Heritage list, but the shape of what is seen today is quite different from the original castle established by the Landgraves of Thuringia in the 11th and 12th centuries. The main part dates from the mid-1100s, but renovations and remodelling over the centuries have changed the look of the castle. In the late medieval period, large parts of the Vorburg — the front part of the castle — were added, but extensive reconstruction in the 19th century is responsible for changing the character from militaristic to romantic.

During its early period, the famous Contests of Wartburg took place and these were also known as the Contests of the Minstrels or Minnesängers. They were held annually in the Sängersaal — the singing room — and a prize was given for the best poem. About 150 of these poems have survived.

The Grand Hall was severely damaged by fire in 1318 and, after this, was given a flat ceiling, but during the 19th century renovations, the composer Franz Liszt suggested a trapezoid design to enhance acoustics. It worked wonders and the hall is still used for concerts and theatrical performances.

Central Germany has a rich cultural heritage, idyllic countryside and delightful towns and villages. Perhaps this is why Johann Sebastian Bach — indeed, almost the entire Bach dynasty of musicians — didn't venture beyond the Thuringian region. The extent of his travels are bounded by Lübeck in the north, Carlsbad in the south, Dresden in the east and Kassel in the west.

A covered external staircase takes visitors up the original main tower of the Wartburg at Eisenach.

RIGHT: Statues of the German poets Schiller and Goethe in front of the Deutsches Nationaltheater in Weimar. The monument was created in 1857 by the German sculptor Ernst Rietschel.

BELOW: On 17 October 1707, Johann Sebastian married his second cousin, Maria Barbara, in this church in the village of Dornheim.

After living with his organist brother for five years, in 1700 Bach moved to Lüneburg where he sang, as a boy soprano, in the choir of the Michaeliskirche — St Michael's Church. This was a paid position which funded his tuition at the Latin school, but by the time he left Lüneburg, two years later, Bach had already composed a number of works for the organ and was developing a passion for church music. It's recorded that he walked great distances to hear renowned musicians of the day play — including 30 miles to Hamburg where the revered organist Johann Adam Reinken was resident at the Katharinenkirche.

At the age of 18, Johann Sebastian went to Arnstadt to test a new organ — made by Herr Wender from the neighbouring village of Mühlhausen — installed in the town's Neue Kirche (New Church). His talent as an organist immediately apparent, he was offered a permanent position. The House of the Palm Tree in Arnstadt is now a museum which houses the actual keyboard and frame of the Wender organ. Only a handful of original 'Bach organs' have survived intact.

While at Arnstadt, Bach began to develop as a composer of organ music, but he also fell foul of the church authorities for, among other things, neglecting the choir, improvising during the hymns and taking extra leave... although a three month's extension is probably worthy of some sort of reprimand! He was also criticised for allowing a "strange maiden" to sing in the choir which was definitely not permitted in those days. The 'mystery woman' was almost certainly Bach's second cousin,

Maria Barbara, whom he later married in the neighbouring village of Dornheim.

Another village in this region which has played a significant role in Bach history is Wechmar. Johann Sebastian Bach's great great grandfather, Veit, arrived here in 1600 from Hungary. He was a musician too, but established a flour mill and bakery in the village with his son, Johannes. The old bakery at Wechmar is now a museum devoted to Bach family history and, more generally, Thuringian musicians and instrument makers. On display are family documents, portraits and furniture covering the 260-year period that the family lived in Wechmar. There is also a Bach family tree which lists over 1400 names, the direct lineage finally dying out in the 1870s.

WEIMAR

Weimar, on the river Ilm, is the provincial capital of Thuringia and for hundreds of years was the heart of Germany, both politically and culturally. This is where many of the great names in art and culture lived, including the poets Schiller, Goethe and Herder; the composers Franz Liszt and Richard Strauss, and the philosopher Nietzsche. Many famous writers and artists were associated with the Bauhaus School which was founded in Weimar in 1919.

Bach lived here too — twice, in fact. The first time was for just a few months before taking up his organist's position at Arnstadt, but the second

ABOVE: Angling in Weimar's Ilm River.

OPPOSITE: Now a museum, the Schillerhaus in Weimar is where Friedrich Schiller wrote William Tell *in 1804.*

time he stayed for nine years from 1708 to 1717. The devout Lutheran duke of Weimar, Wilhelm Ernst, hired Bach as organist and, encouraged to explore his virtuoso techniques and ideas, he developed both as a player and a composer. Some of his greatest organ works — such as the *Prelude and Fugue in D* — come from this period.

He also wrote many cantatas, including the first in a new Italian style, adopted in 1713 and influenced by Vivaldi's concertos, some of which Bach transcribed into organ music.

Four of Johann Sebastian's children were baptised in the Church of St. Peter and St. Paul at Weimar. Its famous altar paintings are by Lucas Cranach the Elder who knew Martin Luther and painted a number of portraits of the reformer.

For a young man still in his 20s, Johann Sebastian was by now well paid and already becoming more widely known, being described by a music writer of the time as "the famous organist of Weimar". He even turned down a significant job offer — to become the organist at the Liebfrauenkirche in Halle — after Duke Wilhelm Ernst promptly doubled his salary in response. In return, though, Bach was required to write one cantata a month.

Bach's relationship with his employer was apparently cordial, but after refusing to observe a ban on providing any musical services to the duke's rival and co-ruler, Johann Sebastian was overlooked for the coveted job of *kapellmeister* after the incumbent died. Greatly offended, he decided to accept the position of *kapellmeister* for Prince Leopold von Anhalt-Köthen, in the city of Köthen. Wilhelm Ernst reacted by having Bach arrested and imprisoned for a month, after which his was summarily dismissed "without honour". Not surprisingly, the composer wasted no time moving to Köthen and his new position.

For a comparatively small place, Weimar is rich in both history and the arts. This is primarily as a result of the efforts of Duke Carl Augustus or, to be more precise, his wife Anna Amalia. Just 19 years old when she became the Duchess of Weimar in 1759, Anna Amalia was both highly educated and an art lover. One of her first actions as the Duchess was to establish a library at Weimar in a former Mannerist palace which has one of the finest Rococo interiors in Europe.

Anna hired the poet and philosopher Christoph Wieland as a tutor for her son, Carl August. Wieland educated the boy in literature and the arts which he believed led to moral enlightenment. Carl August enthusiastically adopted this philosophy and, after coming of age, he carried on where his mother — who retired into private life at the grand old age of 35 — had left off. He invited the poet and writer Johann Wolfgang von Goethe to

Weimar to take up the post of Secretary of State. Within a short time Friedrich Schiller had also moved here and many others, all attracted by the duke's promotion and support of the arts. Many of the houses where these artists and philosophers once lived are now museums. Schiller's house is a late Baroque building, built 300 years ago, and it's where he wrote *Wilhelm Tell* in 1804. The Hungarian-born composer Franz Liszt lived in the former court gardener's quarters — on the top floor — for 14 years and, during the summer months, taught students who came from all over Europe. The room where he composed the *Hungarian Rhapsodies* is preserved.

Goethe's house was presented to him by Carl Augustus and it's where the poet produced his most famous work, *Faust*. Goethe also had a summer house, alongside the river Ilm, which can also be visited today.

After suffering a mental breakdown in Turin, Friedrich Nietzsche was close to insane when he came to Weimar and spent his last three years in a house on Humboldtstrasse, dying in 1900. The restored Art Nouveau building now houses the Nietzsche Archive, but many of his original manuscripts are in the town's Anna Amalia Library.

It's ironic that Nietzsche — the man whose philosophies of "God is dead" and the "Superman" so inspired Adolf Hitler in his desire to dominate the world — should have died in this town. The appalling outcome of Hitler's ideas can be seen at the former Nazi concentration camp of Buchenwald, about eight kilometres north of Weimar.

Leipzig

…Music served its purpose, had its day, and then effectively vanished; in the case of the St Matthew Passion, it vanished for nearly a century. It took a young man from a Jewish family to ignite a fresh interest in Bach's music with a performance of the St Matthew Passion eighty years after the composer's death. Mendelssohn was his name…

SIMON CALLOW

J.S. Bach spent six years in Köthen and during this time, in 1720, Maria Barbara died after a short illness. He was away in Carlsbad and wasn't informed about his wife's death until he returned. He subsequently married Anna Magdalena Wilcke who was an accomplished soprano and, at 20, 16 years his junior. She was to bear Johann Sebastian 13 children as well as being step-mother to the four surviving children from his first marriage. Sadly, eight of them died, but the youngest son, Johann Christian, went on to become a successful composer in his own right.

In 1723, Bach moved to Leipzig to take up the position of *kantor* at the Thomasschule (incidentally, after Georg Philipp Telemann — Germany's most famous composer at the time — turned down the job). Situated in the eastern German state of Saxony, Leipzig was granted town status in 1165 and its university was established in 1409. Over the centuries it became one of Germany's most important commercial centres, notably for book publishing, and the German National Library (Deutsche Bücherei) was established here in 1912. The city's *alt städt* (old town) centre provides many fine examples of Gothic, Baroque and Renaissance architecture.

Bach was hugely prolific while in Leipzig, producing some of his most famous works, both sacred and secular, including the *Magnificat*, *St Matthew Passion*, *St John Passion*, the *Christmas Oratorio* and the *Easter Oratorio*. In his early years in the city, Bach is said to have written one cantata every week, although only a little over half have survived (his total lifetime's output of known musical works is put at over 970). In 1729, J.S. Bach was appointed director of the Collegium Musicum — at the University of Leipzig — which had been founded in 1702 by Telemann. The Collegium played regularly at a coffee house on Katharinenstrasse which led Bach to write the *Coffee Cantata* — possibly one of the earliest advertising jingles!

During the last decade of his life Bach visited Berlin on a number of occasions and, in 1747, was received by King Frederick The Great of Prussia. A keen amateur musician, the King gave Bach a theme which he reworked to produce the *Musical Offering*. Bach's last great work, the *B Minor Mass*, was completed in 1749. Increasingly suffering from cataracts in his latter years (likely to have been caused by diabetes), Johann Sebastian Bach died of a stroke in Leipzig on 28 July 1750 and his tomb is now in the chancel of St Thomas church, outside of which stands a two-and-a-half metre statue of the composer. However, initially Bach was buried in an unmarked grave in the Old St John's Cemetery, something which appalled Felix Mendelssohn when he visited the city nearly

PREVIOUS PAGES: The concert hall in Leipzig's Neues Gewandhaus. The original Gewandhaus was badly damaged in WW2 and eventually demolished in 1968.
INSET: Niki Vasilakis in the Thomaskirche where J.S. Bach was kapellmeister from 1723 to 1729.

OPPOSITE: The Neues Opernhaus in Leipzig. The original opera house dates back to 1693 and a new one was built in 1868, but this building was destroyed in WW2. The current building was opened in 1960.

ABOVE: Where to stand when viewing sites in Leipzig related to J.S. Bach's time in the city. He was here from 1723 to 1750.

ABOVE: The Thomaskirche (St Thomas's Church) is a late-Gothic design built from 1482 to 1496. In 1723 J.S. Bach got the job as choirmaster here after Georg Telemann – who was offered the position first – decided to stay in Hamburg.

80 years later. A naturally gifted musician, Mendelssohn conducted the second ever performance of Bach's *St Matthew Passion* in 1829 while still only 20. This event is said to have led to a 19th century revival of Bach's music and Mendelssohn maintained many of the classical forms and ideas in his composing. Born into a wealthy Jewish family which later converted to Christianity, Felix Bartholdy Mendelssohn was well educated, including a period in Paris while still a child, and became proficient on the violin, piano and organ, as well as in composing and conducting. His first public performance — as a pianist — was in 1818 in Berlin when Felix was just nine. He became the music director of the Leipzig Gewandhaus in 1835, following extensive tours of Europe and a period of time in Düsseldorf. His influence was considerable, so much so that during this time Leipzig was essentially Germany's music capital. He founded the city's Conservatory in 1843. A room in the Altes Rathaus — the Old Town Hall — is devoted to the composer who sadly died young, suffering a series of strokes when aged 38 and while still in charge of the Gewandhaus orchestra. He is buried in Berlin's Friedhöfe vor dem Halleschen Tor. Despite his comparatively short life, Mendelssohn left behind a wealth of work which combined elements of both the classical and romantic eras, but it is his talent for orchestration — as evidenced in symphonies such as the 'Scottish' (*Symphony No. 3 in A minor*) and the 'Italian' (*Symphony No. 4 in A major*) — which elevate him to greatness.

Built in 1556, Leipzig's Old Town Hall — considered one of Germany's most beautiful Renaissance buildings — also houses a room dedicated to J.S. Bach.

Scenes from around Leipzig; a window display of Bach-related publications, the newly completed stadium (built for the 2006 FIFA Football World Cup). The Rathaus (Town Hall) and the fountain in front of the Neues Gewandhaus concert hall.

LEIPZIG AT A GLANCE

WEBSITE – www.leipzig.de

COMPOSERS – Georg Philipp Telemann, Johann Sebastian Bach, Johann Christian Bach, Felix Mendelssohn-Bartholdy, Robert Schumann, Clara (Wieck) Schumann, Edvard Grieg, Gustav Mahler, Richard Wagner.

POPULATION – 497,330.

CLIMATE

WINTER – generally mild, although can be below freezing, average temperature is 0 degrees Celsius, January and February are the coldest months, moderate snowfall.

SPRING – generally warming up towards the end of March, although can sometimes be cool until the beginning of May. Temperatures range between 10 and 20 degrees Celsius. Weather can be quite mixed and changeable during April.

SUMMER – warm with an average temperature of 18 degrees Celsius, but maximum temperatures can exceed 30 degrees Celsius during July and August.

AUTUMN – generally mild until the middle of October, but cool nights. Average daytime temperatures between 15 and 20 degrees Celsius. November is often misty and wet.

BEST TIME OF THE YEAR TO VISIT – March to December.

TOP FIVE TOURIST ATTRACTIONS

ST. THOMAS'S CHURCH (Thomaskirche) – with Bach's grave, and the St. Thomas's Boys Choir (Thomanerchor) which sings at services on Friday, Saturday and Sunday.

AUERBACHS KELLER – made famous by Goethe's Faust.

SEPTEMBER CONCERTS in the Leipzig Gewandhaus, Augustus Platz 8.

THE GIANT MONUMENT to the 1813 Battle of the Nations.

LEIPZIG ZOO (in the Rosental Park).

TOP TWO COFFEE HOUSES

Zum Arabischen Coffe Baum (also a coffee museum)

Café Kandler

MUST SEE SHOPPING LOCATIONS

Hauptbahnhof Promenaden – a mall inside Leipzig's central railway station.

Mädler Passage city arcade.

COMPOSERS MUSEUMS /HOMES

THE BACH MUSEUM in the Bosehaus, Thomaskirchhof 15-16. In addition to an extensive of archive of documents relating to J.S Bach's works, this museum also contains a collection of period musical instruments.

MENDELSSOHN HOUSE, Goldschmidtstrasse 12.

CLARA AND ROBERT SCHUMANN HOUSE, Inselstrasse 18.

EDVARD GRIEG MEMORIAL PLACE.

GARDENS/PARKS MUST SEE

Rosental Park (including Leipzig Zoo).

Clara Zetkin Park (including Franz Schubert Platz).

Johanna Park (on Lassalle Strasse).

Botanical Garden of Leipzig University.

ANNUAL MUSICAL EVENTS

April – The 'a capella' Festival of Vocal Music, www.dreieck-marketing.de

May – The Leipzig Bach Festival, www.bach-leipzig.de

July and August – Monday evening concerts at the Bach Statue in front of the Thomaskirche, www.event-ag-leipzig.de

September – Schumann Festival Week, www.schumann-verein.de

September/October – Mendelssohn Festival, www.gewandhaus.de

October – The Festival of Early Music, www.festtage.net

October – Leipzig Jazz Festival, www.jazzclub-leipzig.de

November – International Festival of Chamber Music, www.kammermusikfestivalleipzig.de

December – Bach's Christmas Oratorio at the Gewandhaus and other churches in Leipizg, www.gewandhaus.de

Easter – Bach's Passions (Thursday, Friday and Saturday)

All Year – Sunday concerts at the Mendelssohn-Haus, www.mendelssohn-stiftung.de

INFORMATION AND TICKETS

Leipzig Tourist Service, Richard-Wagner-Strasse 1, D04109 Leipzig. Telephone +49 (0) 341 710 4260, email Info@LTS-Leipzig.de or visit www.leipzig.de

During his time in Leipzig, Mendelssohn became friends with Robert Schumann who had also enjoyed a privileged upbringing and exhibited musical gifts from an early age. It was intended he become a lawyer and so was enrolled at Leipzig University in 1828, but subsequently decided to become a musician and joined the household of a renowned piano teacher, Friedrich Wieck. There he encountered the 11-year-old Clara Wieck, a child prodigy, with whom he fell in love, eventually marrying her in 1840 (the day before she turned 21). The apartment where the couple lived, at Inselstrasse 18, had two grand pianos and was the scene of many parties attended by, among others, Mendelssohn, Liszt, Chopin and Berlioz. Schumann taught composition and piano at the newly-established Leipzig Conservatory, although it's recorded he was ineffective and absent-minded. The latter may well have been the result of deteriorating mental health which eventually led to a nervous breakdown, a suicide attempt and admittance to an asylum near Bonn where, in 1856 and after two-and-a-half years, he died aged 46. Intensity was clearly a characteristic of Schumann's life and it's evident in the imaginative nature of his compositions, especially the later symphonies (such as the 'Rhenish' — *Symphony No.3 in E flat*), and the animation of his numerous piano works.

The 1908 Sauer organ inside the Thomaskirche. Only a keyboard survives from Bach's time here.

The St Thomas Church school in Leipzig has another important link with classical music. Eighty years after Bach worked there, a pupil was the

ABOVE: Richard Wagner was born in Leipzig and educated at the Thomasschule where, a century earlier, J.S. Bach had been the choirmaster.

RIGHT: Friedrich Wieck not only taught the piano, he sold them. This example is in the Robert Schumann Haus in Leipzig. Schumann became Wieck's pupil in 1830 and, ten years later, married his daughter, Clara (who became a noted composer in her own right).

OPPOSITE: Inside the Mendelssohnhaus. In 1835, Felix Mendelssohn became musical director of the original Leipzig Gewandhaus which triggered a renaissance in musical activity in the city.

teenage Richard Wagner who was born in Leipzig in 1813. He studied literature as well as music, a combination that subsequently influenced his work which has been described as "music drama". He composed his one and only symphony when 19, but his passion was for opera, an inspiration which came from seeing a performance of Beethoven's *Fidelio*. He created his own style of opera, often based on poetry and epic in duration. The longest, *Der Ring Des Nibelungen* (more commonly known simply as 'The Ring'), is a cycle of four operas which runs over four nights and took 25 years to complete. Wagner's first successful opera, *Der Fliegende Holländer (The Flying Dutchman)*, was staged in Dresden in 1843 which led to his appointment as court opera conductor. After participating in an anti-monarchist uprising, he was forced to flee, first to Weimar (where he stayed with Franz Liszt) and then to Zurich. By all accounts Wagner possessed a foul temper, was entirely self-obsessed, unfaithful to his first wife (the actress Minna Planer) and continually in debt. However, this didn't appear to deter 'Mad' King Ludwig II of Bavaria who was sufficiently taken by the composer to pay off all his debts, house him and provide the funds to finish *The Ring*. The cycle was first performed in 1876 at the Festspielhaus in the northern Bavarian town of Bayreuth. This opera house was designed by Wagner — who ensured it had a stage big enough for his epic productions — and built on donated land with funds raised through subscriptions. The Wagner Festival is still held every July at the opera house. It's worth noting that the audience for the first staging of *The Ring* included the composers Edvard Grieg and Peter Tchaikovsky, and the philosopher Friedrich Nietzsche. Wagner died in Venice in 1883 and is buried in the garden of

Villa Wahnfried, the home in Bayreuth where he had lived with his second wife, Cosima.

The daughter of Franz Liszt, Cosima was married to the conductor Hans von Bülow when Wagner met and pursued her. Liszt was born in Hungary in 1811 and was a gifted pianist who, by the age of 12, had already performed around Europe. He's acknowledged as pioneering the solo piano recital performed from memory, and of establishing the form of the 'symphonic poem'. In 1847 Liszt was appointed *kapellmeister* at the Weimar court where, incidentally, he conducted the first performance of Wagner's opera *Lohengrin*. Towards the end of his life Liszt took minor holy orders, becoming an abbé and composing mostly church music. His last years were spent in Bayreuth where his home is now a museum.

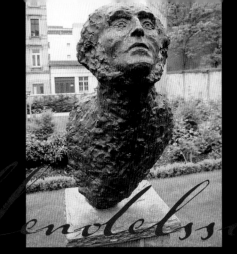

FELIX MENDELSSOHN AT A GLANCE

Born Jacob Ludwig Felix Mendelssohn-Bartholdy on 3 February 1809 in Hamburg, he is a rarity among Romantic era composers in that his family were wealthy and he would never have to struggle to make a living. Nevertheless, young Felix was also wealthy in terms of natural talent. He made his concert debut (in Berlin) when aged only nine and was already composing works for instruments and voices.

Despite his innate abilities, Mendelssohn was made to study hard, not just in music, but also in art and poetry. When aged 17, he wrote his overture to *A Midsummer's Night Dream*, originally as a piano duet, but orchestrated a year later and today one of his most popular works.

In 1821 Mendelssohn had his first meeting with Goethe, subsequently becoming the poet's protégé.

After he was given a copy of Bach's *St Matthew Passion* by his grandmother (the family converted from Judaism to Christianity in 1816), he became the second only person to conduct the oratorio, triggering a revival of the great composer's music.

In 1829 Mendelssohn made the first of ten visits to Britain where, in Scotland, he met Sir Walter Scott and was inspired to write his *Hebrides Overture* (also known as 'Fingal's Cave'). The subsequent visits led to the famous 'Scottish' symphony (*No.3 in A minor*) which was dedicated to Queen Victoria and first performed in 1842.

In 1835, Mendelssohn was appointed musical director of the Leipzig Gewandhaus and his energy and talent soon began to attract musicians to the city. In 1836, his first oratorio, *St Paul*, was presented in Düsseldorf and, a year later, performed in Birmingham. That same year he married a French woman, Cécile Jeanrenaud, who was ten years his junior and would bear him five children.

In 1841, and at the request of the Prussian Emperor Frederick William IV, he was appointed *kapellmeister* and moved to Berlin where he was to eventually head the music department of the Academy of Arts. When this failed to eventuate he was released to return to Leipzig where a more successful project, the Conservatory, was established in 1843. A second oratorio, *Elijah*, was premiered in Birmingham in 1846 to great acclaim, conducted by Mendelssohn himself.

However, by now the punishing workload that he had been undertaking for many years was beginning to take its toll on his health. The death of his much-loved sister, Fanny, with whom he had performed as teenager, exacerbated his frail condition. Not long after returning to Leipzig from Berlin he suffered a series of strokes and died on 4 November 1847, aged only 38. It's a testimony to how much was accomplished in just 30 years that, today, Felix Mendelssohn's contribution to classical composition is recognised for its significance.

Berlin

Bonn

…The end of the
Ninth Symphony is after all,
an Ode To Joy, its unforgettable central
theme called on when footballers win the
World Cup, when the Berlin Wall falls, at any
time people want to express earth-and
heaven-storming elation…

SIMON CALLOW

*S*uch were Liszt's talents that he was said to have been kissed by an admiring Beethoven which is quite a tribute from the man who vies with Bach and Mozart for the title of 'the greater composer who ever lived'.

Ludwig van Beethoven was born in the German city of Bonn in 1770. The capital of the Federal Republic of Germany from 1949 to 1991, Bonn is sited on the Rhine river, not far from Cologne, and was originally founded by the Romans in the 12th century. It's a city rich in history, music, architecture and the arts. Bonn's cathedral, the Münsterbasilika, dates back to 1150 and is a fine example of the so-called 'Rhenish' style which is peculiar to the Rhineland region and was a transition between Romanesque and Gothic.

A statue of Beethoven was unveiled in the Münsterplatz in 1845 on what would have been the composer's 75th birthday, and his *Missa Solemnis* (Mass in D) was performed in the cathedral. In attendance were Franz Liszt (who helped raise funds for the statue), the French composer Hector Berlioz, Queen Victoria and Prince Albert, and the King and Queen of Prussia.

The 18th century Baroque house where Beethoven was born and lived for 22 years is now, not surprisingly, a museum. The Beethovenhaus contains an extensive collection of manuscripts, documents and memorabilia.

Beethoven came from a musical family — his grandfather was the *kapellmeister* of the Elector's court and his father was a tenor in the choir. By the time he was nine, the young Beethoven had already performed his first concert and, when aged 12, his first composition was published. At 13 he too joined the Bonn court, as a harpsichordist. Here he was taught

by the court organist, Christian Gottlob Neefe, displaying sufficient talent to become his deputy and, at 17, sent to Vienna where he briefly studied under Mozart. Impressed with Beethoven's ability, Mozart is said to have commented, "Keep your eye on him; one day he will make the world talk of him".

When his mother, Maria Magdelena, became seriously ill, Beethoven returned to Bonn and she died shortly after. With his father incapacitated by alcoholism, the teenage Ludwig had to care for his two younger brothers and the

PREVIOUS PAGES: The Münster St Martin, Bonn's cathedral, was built from the period 1150 to 1230 in the Romanesque style of the Rhine Valley. INSET: Niki Vasilakis plays in the Grand Hotel Petersburg in Bonn.

OPPOSITE: Inside the Chamber Music Hall built beside the Beethovenhaus with a window that looks out over the composer's garden.

ABOVE: The Beethovenhaus is where the composer was born in December 1770 and lived until he was 22. Naturally, today it's a museum.

LEFT: This graphic sculpture of Beethoven's head (called the 'Beethon') is made from concrete and designed to be viewed from a distance for the full three-dimensional effect. It was created by Klaus Kammerichs in 1986.

family lived at Rheingasse 26 until the home was destroyed after the Rhine burst its banks. He supported the family by teaching and playing the viola in the court orchestra. In 1792, Beethoven, still only 22, was released from court duties and again travelled to Vienna where his teachers were Joseph Haydn and Antonio Salieri (a rival to Mozart who, a year earlier, had died aged just 35). Haydn and Beethoven first met in Bonn in July 1792 at the then newly completed La Redoute concert hall, ballroom and casino. Today, the Beethoven Hall in La Redoute is still used for concerts.

Beethoven never returned to Bonn although other members of the family remained in the area and a Beethoven Festival is held in the city every September. One branch of the family established a vineyard on the banks of the Moselle river, and Beethoven wines can be enjoyed to this day.

Despite his immense talent — or perhaps because of it — history records Ludwig van Beethoven as another of classical music's 'difficult personalities'. He reputedly had an appalling temper, could never settle (occupying 33 lodgings over 35 years), deliberately dressed like

The German National Museum of Contemporary History (Haus der Geschichte der Bundesrepublik Deutschland) in Bonn traces the history of Germany from 1945 up to the reunification.

tramp and pursued relationships with women who were either married or socially superior (or both). It's also well documented that he was tormented by increasing and incurable deafness. By the start of the 19th century he was forced to give up the concert stage and concentrate on composing, but this resulted in some of his greatest works — the third, fourth and fifth piano concertos; his only opera, *Fidelio*; the *Violin Concerto*

BONN AT A GLANCE

WEBSITE – www.bonn.de

COMPOSERS – Ludwig van Beethoven, Robert Schumann.

POPULATION – 313,000.

CLIMATE

WINTER – average daily temperatures range from -1.0 to 4.5 degrees Celsius. Frosts are common in mid-winter.

SPRING – average daily temperatures range from 10 to 17 degrees Celsius.

SUMMER – daily average temperatures range from 15 to 25 degrees Celsius, but mid-summer days can be warmer. High humidity is common during mid-to-late summer. This season can also be rainy.

AUTUMN – daily average temperatures range from 7.0 to 16 degrees Celsius.

BEST TIME OF THE YEAR TO VISIT – Spring and autumn provide the best climate, but classical music lovers shouldn't miss the Beethoven Festival (September to October).

TOP FIVE TOURIST ATTRACTIONS

KUNST — und Ausstellungshalle der Bundesrepublik Deutschland (the Art and Exhibition Hall of the Federal Republic of Germany) – dramatic contemporary buildings showing major exhibitions (visit www.kah-bonn.de for calendar of events).

KUNSTMUSEUM BONN (Bonn Art Museum) – contains a huge collection of 20th century art including many works from the Expressionist period.

MÜNSTER ST MARTIN – magnificent Romanesque cathedral, built from 1150 to 1230.

RATHAUS (Old Town Hall) in the Marktplatz – late-Baroque building in Bonn's classic market square

RHINE RIVER CRUISES – experience some of the most picturesque stretches of this famous river, including vineyards and historic castles.

TOP TWO COFFEE HOUSES

Café Fassbender, Sternstrasse 55 (Bonn city centre).

Bon(n) Gout, Remigiusplatz 2–4 (Bonn city centre).

MUST SEE SHOPPING LOCATIONS

Kaiserpassage – a pedestrian precinct in Bonn's city centre which contains many fashionable boutiques, department stores and specialty shops.

COMPOSERS MUSEUMS/HOMES

BEETHOVENHAUS (Beethoven House) – the 18th century Baroque house where Beethoven was born and lived until he was 22. Houses an extensive collection of memorabilia. At Bonngasse 24–26

SCHUMANNHAUS (Schumann House) – memorial rooms in a former psychiatric hospital, where Robert Schumann stayed from 1854 until his death in summer of 1856. At Sebastianstrasse 182.

GARDENS/PARKS MUST SEE

POPPELSDORFER SCHLOSS (Poppelsdorf Palace) – Baroque palace (actually called Clemensruhe Schloss) surrounded by formal gardens and extensive parklands. Poppelsdorf is a southwestern suburb of Bonn.

ANNUAL MUSICAL EVENTS

September/October – Beethoven Festival; over 50 concerts with renowned stars and orchestras staged at various venues around Bonn, including the Steigenberger Grandhotel Petersberg in Königswinter, www.beethovenfest.de

INFORMATION

Bonn Information, Windeckstrasse 2 (near Münsterplatz), 53111 Bonn, telephone +49 (0)228 775 000, www.bonn-region.de

in D; four symphonies (including No.6, the *'Pastoral'*) and the stirring *Ode to Joy* finale to his *Symphony No.9 in D minor* (the rest of it then yet to be written) set for Schiller's poem of the same name. Not surprisingly, after this highly productive period, Beethoven's output declined, but in his latter years — now totally deaf — his inspiration returned and his music embodied more of a spiritual element, including the *Missa Solemnis* and the iconic ninth symphony, the *'Choral'*. Fittingly, a fierce storm was raging over Vienna when Ludwig van Beethoven died, and a loud thunder clap is said to have stirred the composer to raise a defiant fist as he took his last breath.

After the reunification of the two post-war Germanys in 1990, Berlin was restored as the nation's capital and most government departments transferred from Bonn (which was compensated and has subsequently flourished as a commercial centre). Berlin's history dates back to a small fishing village established on the banks of the Spree river in 1237. It first became a capital — of the Brandenburg region — in 1486 and grew rapidly during the 16th century, notably converting to Martin Luther's Protestantism in 1539. In 1701 Berlin became the capital of the kingdom of Prussia, and King Friedrich I encouraged both the arts and sciences. After Napoleon defeated Prussia in 1806, Berlin was occupied by the French for two years. It became the capital of the German Empire in 1871 and was the venue for the 1936 Olympic Games, sadly marred by Adolf Hitler's relentless promotion of Aryan supremacy. After World War II, the 1945 Potsdam Conference divided Berlin into four sectors, occupied by the British,

OPPOSITE: Bonn's late-Baroque Rathaus (Town Hall) was built in 1737.

BELOW: Beethoven's statue in Bonn's Münsterplatz. It was largely paid for by Liszt with a combination of his own finances and the proceeds from concerts. It was unveiled in 1845.

OPPOSITE: Das Brandenburger Tor – the Brandenburg Gate – was built from 1788 to 1791 and has come to be symbolic of Berlin. It was dismantled by Napoleon in 1806 and returned in 1814. From 1945 it was in East Berlin. It has now been fully restored. Seen here is part of the Quadriga sculpture which crowns the structure.

BELOW: The recreation of the famous 'Checkpoint Charlie' border crossing point between East and West Berlin. Erected in 1961, the Berlin Wall was torn down in 1989 and the two Germanys reunified on 3 October 1990. A nearby museum – the Haus am Checkpoint Charlie – documents many of the escape attempts.

US, French and Soviet troops. In June 1948, the Soviets attempted to annex Berlin by blockading the western sectors which led the allies to airlift in all supplies for nearly a year. The Federal Republic of Germany — with Bonn as its capital — was established in 1949, and Berlin remained a city divided, literally by a wall after 1961, for 40 years. The Berlin Wall was finally breached on 9 November 1989 and Germany officially reunified on 3 October 1990.

Berlin's links to classical music are numerous and the city is home to several professional symphony orchestras, including the one considered the world's finest — the Berlin Philharmonic. Its home is in the Philharmonie which was designed by Hans Scharoun and is part of the Kulturforum complex, built to replace the venues lost to East Berlin after the wall went up. Like many German cities heavily damaged by Allied bombing, Berlin has a reconstructed old quarter. The Nikolaiviertel — St. Nicholas Quarter — replicates the atmosphere of old Berlin, but just one original Baroque building survived the war, a small townhouse built in 1759 for the Knoblauch family. The Nikolaikirche is Berlin's oldest church, although all that's left of the original is the base of a façade which dates from around 1300. Destroyed by bombing in 1945, rebuilding of the church was finally completed in 1987.

Born in Munich, Richard Strauss was conductor of the Royal Opera in Berlin from 1898 to 1917, and his controversial career included the appointment as director of the Reichsmusikkammer after the Nazi Party came to power in 1933. However, two years later he was removed from the post after a collaboration with the Jewish librettist, Stefan Zweig.

After Hitler was appointed German chancellor in January 1933, a fire at the Reichstag — now widely believed to have been deliberately started by the Nazis — was used as the catalyst to begin ruthlessly crushing opponents. Built at the end of the 19th century to house the German Empire's parliament (and, ironically, paid for by French wartime reparations), the fire-damaged Reichstag wasn't restored until the early 1970s. After reunification, it was extensively remodelled by the British architect Sir Norman Forster, to function as a modern centre of government.

Notable is the elliptical transparent dome incorporating a concentric viewing gallery which provides 360-degree views of the city.

However, perhaps the structure most identified with Berlin is The Brandenburg Gate — in German, Das Brandenburger Tor. Modelled on the entrance to the Acropolis in Athens and built from 1788 to 1791, it was dismantled during the French occupation and transported to Paris, subsequently being returned in 1814 as a symbol of victory. After 1945, it also become symbolic of the east-west divide as did Checkpoint Charlie which was the only crossing point for civilians between West and East Berlin — Charlie representing 'C' in the phonetic alphabet, i.e. the third border post in the Berlin city centre. A total of 1065 people died trying to flee East Berlin and, after the Wall fell in 1989, a celebratory concert was conducted on Christmas Day. Leonard Bernstein conducted Beethoven's ninth symphony with one important change — the finale was renamed *Ode to Freedom*.

Czech Repu

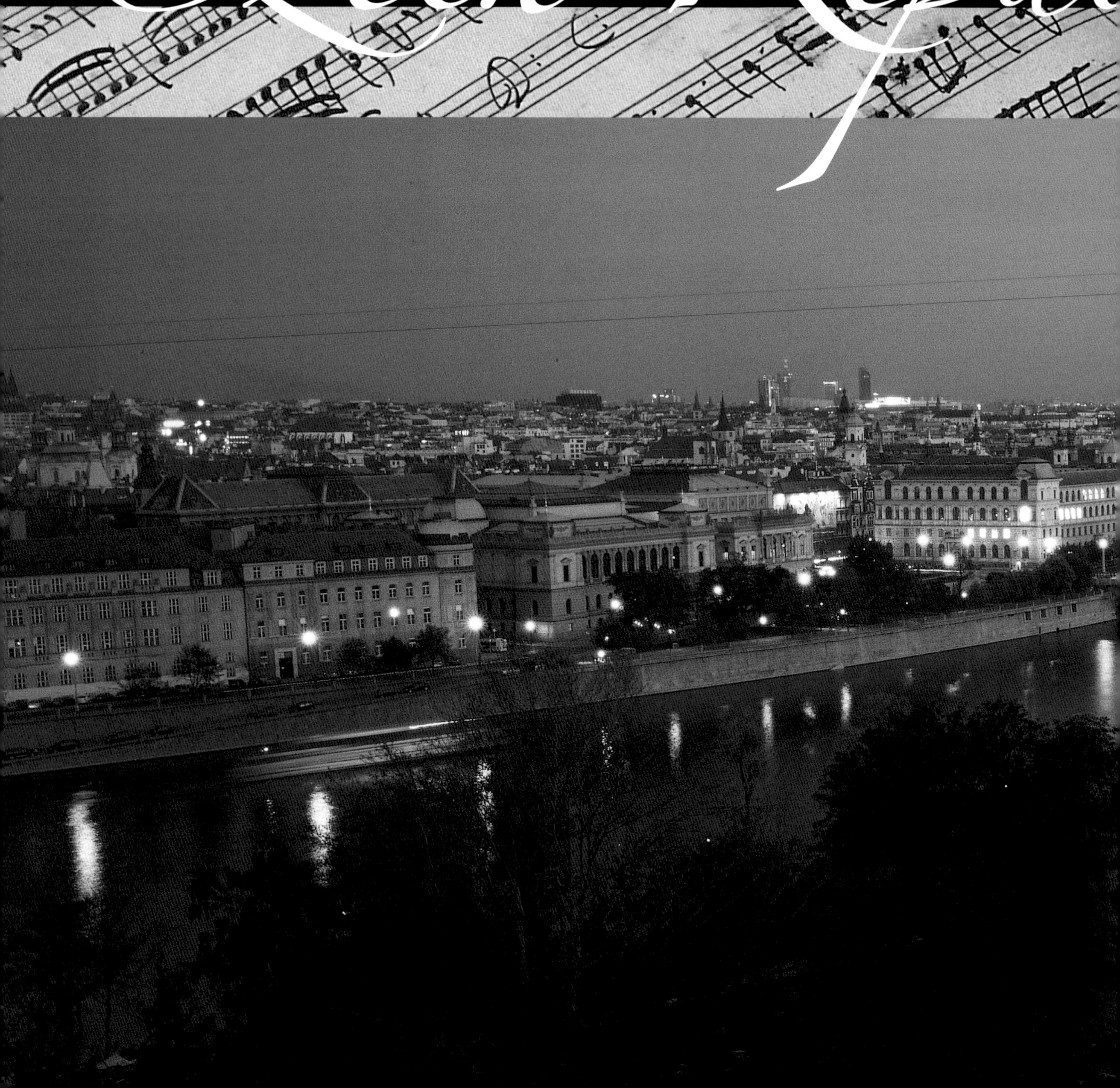

Prague

...Prague is a city of
such striking beauty it's hardly
surprising that one of the greatest Czech
composers — Smetana — wanted to
write music about it. To do so was also
a loud, clear political statement...

SIMON CALLOW

*O*ften called 'The City of a Thousand Spires', Prague was the ancient capital of Bohemia and today is the modern capital of the Czech Republic. It's positioned on the banks of the Vltava River and was established in the ninth century, developing into an important trading centre during the 14th century and an important cultural centre in the late 16th century. These are known as Bohemia's two 'Golden Ages'

One of the early kings of Prague was a pious young man called Prince Václav. Better known now as Good King Wenceslas, he was born in 907 AD and is immortalised in the Christmas carol. He became king when still a young man and was known for his kindness to the poor hence the label 'good'.

However, he came from a highly dysfunctional family and when he tried to rein in the greed of the nobility, they prevailed on his brother Boleslav to help dispose of the young king. Wenceslas, aged only 22, was murdered while on his way to Mass and this act appropriately earned Boleslav the epithet of 'the Cruel'. Wenceslas, on the other hand, became the patron saint of Prague.

The first 'Golden Age' was during the reign of the Holy Roman Emperor Charles IV from 1346 to 1378. Prague flourished under the progressive king and was then bigger than either Paris or London. Charles' legacy is very evident in the city and includes the famous Charles Bridge and St Vitus Cathedral. He also established the first university in Central Europe which today is also named after him.

The first Bohemian rector of the university was a Protestant religious reformer called Jan Hus (or John Huss to use the Anglicised form). Appointed in 1402, his

preaching inspired the nationalistic Hussite movement, but was considered heresy by the Roman Catholic church and, after being excommunicated in 1412, Hus was burned at the stake three years later. Nevertheless, his followers, led by the patriot Ziska, continued to promote his reforms which eventually led to a civil war that lasted from 1419 to 1434... when the Black Death plague intervened.

Established in the 9th century, Prague Castle not only survived many wars and fires, but grew into the largest complex of its kind in the world. It's essentially a small town in its own right and the site includes the cathedral Charles IV founded in 1344, a chancellery building, a basilica and the Convent of St George which today houses a collection of Czech art from the 16th century. Good King Wenceslas lived in what is now

PREVIOUS PAGES: Prague is one of the most beautiful cities in Europe. The many bridges over the River Vltava are pictured here at dusk.
Classical Destinations *TV series co-presenter, Niki Vasilakis, plays the violin on the historic Charles Bridge.*
INSET: Detail of the ornate ceiling in St Nicholas Church.

LEFT: Prague's Old Town with the distinctive twin steeples of the Týn Church seen to the left (and above).

called the Old Royal Palace and his tomb is in a chapel within the cathedral. Today Prague Castle continues to be the seat of power, housing the offices of the President of the Czech Republic. But it's not all business and some of the old ramparts have been replaced by a series of formal gardens.

Only finally completed in 1929, St Vitus' Cathedral is arguably Prague's most distinctive landmark. St Vitus was a young Sicilian martyr who was thrown to the lions during the Roman persecutions. The works of art in the cathedral stretch from the Renaissance through to the early 20th century and include mosaics, stained-glass windows, wall paintings and reliefs. On a door in the Wenceslas Chapel is the bronze Romanesque ring which, according to legend, the King clung to as he was murdered by his brother.

OPPOSITE: St Vitus Cathedral dominates the view of Prague Castle from the Charles Bridge.

ABOVE: A statue of Prince Václav, better known as 'Good' King Wenceslas — of Christmas carol fame — who was renowned for his piety and reigned over Bohemia from 921 to 929.

LEFT: Wenceslas was murdered by his brother Boleslav, appropriately named 'the Cruel'. The slain King's tomb is in a 14th century chapel attached to St Vitus Cathedral.

While the construction of St Vitus Cathedral began in the 14th century, it wasn't finally completed until 1929. Today it dominates the Prague skyline by day and by night.

In 1526, the Catholic Hapsburgs took over Bohemia which led to a counter-Reformation and the beginning of Austrian rule. Rudolf II made Prague the capital of the Hapsburg empire and initiated the second 'Golden Age'. He was a lover of the arts and sciences, and considered instrumental in bringing the Renaissance to Prague. After his death in 1612, Bohemia rejected the next Austrian king and made a bid for independence. The 'Thirty Years War' ended with Austria tightening its grip of Bohemia and initiating a decline which lasted until the 18th century.

During the reign of Empress Maria Theresa many of the Baroque buildings that are still evident in the city were established. The Vladislav Hall, also in the Prague Castle complex, is a magnificent Gothic structure and gives a tremendous feeling for the centuries of activity which took place here. It was where the Royal Court functions were held and which, on a day-to-day basis, was more like a public market than a royal palace.

The 19th century saw a rebirth of national pride in Bohemia and a number of great public monuments were built, including the National Museum — at the southeast end of Prague's famous Wenceslas Square — and the National Theatre. Built in 1881, the theatre was funded by a public collection, but was extensively damaged by fire shortly after it was

PRAGUE AT A GLANCE

WEBSITE: www.prague-info.cz

COMPOSERS: Bedřich Smetana, Antonín Dvořák, Leos Janacek, Wolfgang Amadeus Mozart.

POPULATION: 1,200,000.

CLIMATE

WINTER – average temperatures range from -5 to +5 degrees Celsius.

SPRING – average temperatures range from 10 to 15 degrees Celsius.

SUMMER – daytime temperatures can reach 30 degrees during mid-summer.

AUTUMN – average temperatures range from 8 to 12 degrees Celsius.

TOP FIVE TOURIST ATTRACTIONS

PRAGUE CASTLE (Pražský hrad) – the biggest castle complex in the world and essentially a small town in its own right. Sights include St Vitus Cathedral with the tomb of St Wenceslas.

CHARLES BRIDGE (Karluv most) – Prague's oldest bridge founded by Charles IV in 1357. Features 30 sculptures of the saints.

OLD TOWN (Staré Město) – the Old Town Square includes the gothic Old Town Hall features an astronomical clock and calendarium.

JEWISH QUARTER (Josefov) – includes the Prague Jewish Museum and a holocaust memorial.

MUNICIPAL HOUSE – impressive Art Nouveau building that's now a cultural centre and includes the Smetana Concert Hall.

TOP TWO COFFEE HOUSES

Café Slavia (Kavarna Slavia) – opposite the National Theatre in Nové Město at Smetanovo nábřelí 2.

Café Louvre – once frequented by Kafka, Čapek and Einstein. At Národni třída 20. www.cafelouvre.cz

MUST SEE SHOPPING LOCATIONS

Na příkopě (in Nové Město) – one of Prague's main shopping streets in the 'New Town'.

Wenceslas Square (in Nové Město) – a broad avenue lined with shops and restaurants, and dominated by the statue of St Wenceslas.

COMPOSERS MUSEUMS/HOMES

Antonín Dvořák Museum – housed in a beautiful Baroque summer house and containing documents, memorabilia and pictures. Ke Karlovu 20, Nové Město (New Town). www.nm.cz

Mozart Museum – the full title is actually Bertramka; Museum To W.A. Mozart and Mr and Mrs Dusek. Villa Bertramka was the Dusek's home and it's where Mozart finished *Don Giovanni*. Concerts held here from June to September. Mozartova 169, Smíchov. www.bertramka.cz

Bedřich Smetana Museum – extensive collection of items documenting the composer and conductor's life. Novotného lávka 1, Staré Město (Old Town). www.nm.cz

GARDENS/PARKS MUST SEE

PRAGUE CASTLE GARDENS (Zahrady – Pražský hrad) – royal gardens established in 1534 and opened daily by a fanfare.

PALACE GARDENS UNDER PRAGUE CASTLE – includes the Small and Great Palffy Gardens, Ledebur Garden, the Small Fürstenberg Gardens and Kolowrat.

VRTBOVSKÁ GARDEN (Vrtbovská zahrada) – terraced Baroque gardens including many sculptures by Braun. Karmelitská 25, Malá Strana (Little Quarter).

ANNUAL MUSICAL EVENTS

January – Prague Winter Festival, classical music, opera and ballet. www.praguewinterfestival.com

May to June – Prague Spring Festival, with concerts in various venues around the city. www.festival.cz

June – Musica Sacra Praga, festival of sacred music. www.clubta.cz

July to August – Nightly performances of Mozart's opera Don Giovanni at the Estates Theatre, Staré Město, www.mozart-praha.cz

July to August – Organ Summer, international festival of organ music. www.obecni-dum.cz

August to September – Verdi Festival, Verdi's operas performed at the State Opera Prague. www.sop.cz

September to October - Prague Autumn Festival, international music festival. www.pragueautumn.cz

October to December – Strings Of Autumn, classical music concerts in the halls of Prague Castle. www.strunypodzimu.cz

October – International Jazz Festival. wwwpragokoncert.com

December – International Festival Of Advent And Christmas Music. www.orfea.cz

INFORMATION

Prague Information Service (PIS), Malá Strana Bridge Tower (near Charles Bridge), telephone +420 12 444, www.prague-info.cz

opened. The people gave generously again and the building was finally reopened in 1883 when the festive and patriotic opera *Dalibor a Libuše*, by Bedřich Smetana, was performed.

Today often acknowledged as the father of Czech classical music, Smetana was still a teenager when he wrote in his diary of a desire to be "a Mozart in composition and a Liszt in technique". By all accounts his first attempts at either weren't very successful, but after being appointed piano teacher to a wealthy family and subsequently setting up his own music school, Smetana began to show great promise. His interest in nationalistic themes was sparked by the short-lived revolt against Austrian rule staged in Prague during mid-1848 and brutally repressed. He appears to have struggled with this event although his personal life over the following years was far from happy — three of four daughters born to his wife, Kateřina, died and she was diagnosed with tuberculosis. In 1856 Smetana left Prague for Sweden where he established a music school in Gothenburg. He returned in 1861 and began

pursuing Czech themes, most derived from literature and locations, in his music. It's recorded that his first overtly nationalistic works weren't well received — one accusation being that he was "too Wagnerian" — and he struggled to stage performances. Nevertheless, he hit the right note of patriotic fervour with the populace and his operas, in particular, quickly gained in popularity and remain so in the modern Czech Republic.

ABOVE: Inside Prague's National Theatre. Built with public funds, it was destroyed by fire shortly after it was first completed in 1881. Today it is the venue for operatic, ballet and theatrical productions.

ANTONÍN DVOŘÁK AT A GLANCE

Another 19th century composer who explored nationalistic themes through his music, Antonín Dvořák was born on 8 September 1841 in Nelahozeves, about 30 kilometres north of Prague. As a boy he first learned the violin and was a chorister at the church in Nelahozeves. He also joined the local orchestra and, at a very early age, began composing waltzes and marches. Aged 12, he was sent to live with an uncle in Zlonice where his musical talents came to the attention of his new headmaster, Antonin Liehmann. Also the local organist, he tutored the boy on the viola, piano and organ.

In 1857, now aged 16, Dvořák went to Prague to attend Organ School. He also began playing the viola in orchestras as well as occasionally conducting. In 1862 he joined the newly-formed orchestra of the Czech National Opera and earned a small income teaching music. Dvořák encountered Bedřich Smetana after the latter was appointed the orchestra's conductor and who, by then, was committed to promoting Czech music.

Although Dvořák produced a lot of music through the 1860s – including his first two symphonies – it wasn't until the 1870s that public performances brought any recognition. After playing in the premieres of a number of Smetana's operas, he wrote two of his own – *Alfred* and *King and Collier*. In 1873, Dvořák left the opera orchestra to become the organist at Prague's St Adalbert's church. In the same year,

he married Anna Čermákova who was a church choir contralto. Freed from regular opera performances, Dvořák's creativity and output increased and works from this time include his third and fourth symphonies, the opera *Vanda*, the popular *Serenade for Strings* and the *Symphony No.5 in F major*. His fame began to spread beyond Prague – partly helped by promotion from Brahms – to Germany and beyond to the USA and England.

His popularity was greatly boosted by the *Slavonic Dances* and the *Slavonic Rhapsodies* while his immense talents where revealed in the *Symphony No.6 in D major* (1880), since acknowledged as equal to Beethoven's finest works.

In 1884 Dvořák visited London to conduct the D major symphony at the Albert Hall, returning the next year to present his *Symphony No.7 in D minor* also considered a seminal work. In 1892, he was appointed director of the National Conservatory of Music in New York.

Although composed while he was living in the USA, Dvořák's *Symphony No.9 in E minor* ('From The New World') is still greatly influenced by Czech themes. Homesick, he returned to Prague in 1895 and the last nine years of his life were no less prolific than any other period, producing a number of symphonic poems based on Bohemian themes, a string quartet and three operas.

In 1901, when aged 60, he was appointed director of the Prague Conservatory of Music. Antonín Dvořák died in Prague on 1 May 1904, while sitting at dinner.

Smetana's more notable contributions to the world of classical music include the operas *The Bartered Bride*, *The Kiss* and *The Secret*, and the symphonic poems *Má Vlast* (*My Country*) which include an evocative musical interpretation of the Vltava. Importantly, Smetana influenced later generations of composers, including a member of the National Theatre orchestra which he conducted in the late 1860s. The orchestra's principal viola was a young man called Antonín Leopold Dvořák who had originally come to Prague in 1857 when aged 16 to learn to play organ. However, he was already

LEFT: The neo-Renaissance Rudolfinum was originally designed as an art gallery, and is now the home of the Czech Philharmonic Orchestra.

BELOW: The main concert hall in the Rudolfinum is now called the Dvořák Hall and is the venue for concerts during Prague's many classical music festivals.

proficient on the piano, violin and viola, and as a small boy wrote music for his home village's orchestra.

Once in Prague, Dvořák concentrated on composing and while his output was prolific, by all accounts much of it ended up in the fire. He struggled to earn a living as a teacher and experienced very little success — in terms of recognition, at least — until he was into his early 30s. He supplemented his meagre income by playing the organ at St Adalbert's church in Prague. In 1875 Dvořák applied for an artist's grant from the ruling Austrian government, a process which

ABOVE: Classical Destinations *TV series presenter Simon Callow revisits the streets of Prague's Little Quarter where scenes from the Academy Award winning film* Amadeus — *in which he played the impresario Schikaneder — where filmed.*

RIGHT: *The stairway leading down from Prague Castle to the Little Quarter, also called the Lesser Town or, in Czech, Malá Strana.*

involved submitting compositions. One of the fund's committee members was Johannes Brahms who was sufficiently impressed with the originality of the works to recommend the Bohemian composer to his publishers, Simrock. It also appears that Brahms helped with some business matters, particularly in how to deal with publishers!

Perhaps the most famous of Dvořák's works, the *Slavonic Dances,* were published in 1878 (as piano duets) and brought him immediate acclaim across Europe and in England. This was followed a year later by the third *Slavonic Rhapsody* which was performed in both Berlin and Vienna. Dvořák then enjoyed orchestral success with his *Symphony in D major* which was compared favourably with works by Brahms and Beethoven. He visited London in 1884 to conduct the symphony and other pieces, beginning a long relationship with England which included another eight visits and many commissions. By this time Dvořák was a celebrity and sufficiently well-paid to buy a country home.

He was the recipient of numerous awards and honours, including a professorship of composition at the Prague Conservatory. There was also an honorary doctorate from Cambridge University. In 1892 Dvořák moved to the USA to become head of the New York National Conservatory of Music, a post he first declined but then accepted after persistent badgering from the institution's founder, Mrs Jeannette Thurber who was the wealthy wife of a successful businessman. Antonín and his wife, the singer Anna Čermáková (a former music pupil), and six children lived in the USA for three years, but homesickness led to the composing of his most popular orchestral work, the *Symphony No.9 in E minor (From the*

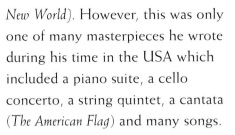

New World). However, this was only one of many masterpieces he wrote during his time in the USA which included a piano suite, a cello concerto, a string quintet, a cantata (*The American Flag*) and many songs.

Dvořák returned to Prague in 1895 and continued his prolific output of material, also conducting at the Rudolfinum in the concert hall that now bears his name. In 1901, at the age of 60, he was appointed director of the Prague Conservatory. Antonín Dvořák died in Prague in 1904, while sitting at dinner, his place in the history of classical music assured. Perhaps more importantly — certainly to Dvořák — he has subsequently been hailed as the greatest of all the Czech composers.

Located beside the Vltava River, the Dvořák Hall in the neo-Renaissance Rudolfinum is, appropriately, the most impressive of Prague's concert halls.

One of the things often said about Prague is that anywhere you point a camera you'll find a great picture. The movie *Amadeus* was filmed almost entirely in the city, primarily because it's been so well preserved and has many public areas and buildings that are still 'Baroque' in their appearance. However, another perhaps more fitting reason that *Amadeus* was filmed in Prague is because, during his lifetime, Mozart was probably more popular in this city than any other.

BEDŘICH SMETANA AT A GLANCE

An inspiration to those that followed him, Bedřich Smetana is often called the 'father of Czech music'. Born on 2 March 1824 in Litomyšl, Bohemia, it's recorded that Smetana played first violin in a Haydn string quartet when aged just five. As a teenager he recorded in his diary that, "I wish to become a Mozart in composition and a Liszt in technique".

In 1843 Smetana moved to Prague to study music and was also appointed piano teacher to the family of Count Leopold Thun. His first experience as a teacher convinced Smetana to establish his own music school in Prague which opened in 1848. He sent his *Six Characteristic Pieces*, written for piano, to Liszt for a critique which was duly supplied.

The first manifestations of Czech nationalism (Bohemia then was under Austrian rule) came with a revolt staged in Prague on 11 June 1848 which was brutally suppressed. This event had a significant impact on Smetana and it was many years before he returned to composing (during which time three of the four daughters born to his wife, Kateřina, died, adding to his distress).

In 1856, he moved to Göteborg in Sweden, recommencing teaching, concert performances (as a pianist) and conducting. A growing interest in exploring Czech themes in his music compelled Smetana to return to Prague in 1861. He returned via Weimar in Germany to visit Liszt who, after playing the *Six Characteristic Pieces*, heralded

Smetana as "an artist". He wasn't so well received at home, though, and was criticised for being too influenced by Wagner. There was even organised opposition to his works, but this changed when his patriotic opera, The *Brandenburgers in Bohemia*, was eventually performed in 1866. This gained him both audience acclaim, and the conductor's position at the Czech National Theatre Orchestra.

The Austro-Prussian war and the threat of invasion forced Smetana to flee Prague, just after the premiere of *The Bartered Bride* which was a huge success and has since become his best-known opera. However, Smetana himself considered it one of his lesser works which was eclipsed by his subsequent operas *The Kiss*, *The Secret* and *Libuše*. Premiered on 11 June 1881 to inaugurate the Czech National Theatre, *Libuše* is Smetana's most patriotic work and celebrated Czech nationhood.

By now the composer was both deaf (an affliction which first appeared in 1874) and in very poor health. Nevertheless, some of Smetana's greatest works were produced during the last decade of his life, including *Má Vlast* (My Country), a cycle of six symphonic poems celebrating the Czech countryside and considered his most important orchestral achievement.

Bedřich Smetana died on 12 May 1884 in Prague, his last days spent in an asylum, but his place in Czech music history assured.

The Villa Bertramka was the home of pianist and composer Frantisek Dusek and his wife, the singer Josefina Duskova. They first staged two of Mozart's operas in Prague and were responsible for inviting him to the city.

The house is now a museum and the strongest link to Mozart's time in Prague. It was here that he finished the score of *Don Giovanni*, supposedly just moments before its opening night at Prague's Estates Theatre on 29 October 1787, conducted by Mozart himself. It's also claimed that he wrote much of *La Clemenza di Tito* while in Prague, and in 1791, this opera also premiered at the Estates Theatre, just weeks before Mozart's death.

During Mozart's time in Prague, the venue was actually called the Nostic Theatre, the name change coming in 1799 when it was acquired by the Czech Estates. In 1834 the theatre was again the location of an important moment in musical — and Czech — history when, on 21 December that year, what would become the country's national anthem was first performed. Derived from an opera by Josef Tyl, *Kde domov muj?* (Where is My Home?), was adopted as the Czech national anthem after the country's liberation in 1918.

The Estates Theatre is in Prague's Old Town and outside stands the brooding statue of the dark Commendatore who, in Mozart's opera, drags the unrepentant, womanising Don Giovanni off to hell. Both Carl Maria von Weber and Gustav Mahler were conductors at this theatre, and Paganini, the famous Italian violinist, gave concerts here.

The salon on the ground floor of Villa Bertramka is where Mozart slept, and today the music room plays host to chamber music concerts. Thanks to the Duseks, Prague grew to love Mozart and he claimed the most beautiful moments of his life were spent at Villa Bertramka. He probably also fondly remembered Bretfeld Palace, on Nerudova Street, where local legend has it, Mozart and Casanova enjoyed some nights together at society balls given by the playboy owner.

CLOCKWISE: The Czech Republic drinks more beer per capita than any other country and boasts some of the world's oldest breweries. The tree-lined Pařizska třída in Prague's Old Town. Enjoying the view from the Charles Bridge which was completed in 1357 – the statues, 30 of them, were added from the 18th century. Stepping back in time in Prague's Old Town Square.

It may come as a surprise to learn that the Czech Republic drinks more beer per capita than any other country in the world! They've been making it at Prague's U Fleku brewery since 1499. The place was bought by Mozart's playboy friend — Jacob Flekovsky — and he called it U Fleku which means "At the Fleks", probably a reference to his nickname. To celebrate 500 years of beer brewing, a museum was established in the old malthouse, and the attached restaurant and beer garden can accommodate up to 1200 revellers. U Fleku is most famous for its 13 percent, dramatically dark coloured beer.

BELOW: The magnificent Baroque church of St Nicholas in the Malá Strana district. A church first stood on this site as far as back as the late 13th century.

Another place associated with Mozart is the Clam-Gallas Palace, also in the Old Town, and partly named after Mathias Gallas de Campo. He acquired the property the 1630s after apparently helping to organise the murder of the previous owner. A grandson was responsible for the reconstruction and expansion which resulted in the large palace compound seen today. In the 18th and early 19th centuries it was a centre for science and the arts in Prague. Both Mozart and Beethoven — among many others — gave concerts at the palace. It's likely Mozart was introduced to the Clam-Gallas household by his friends, the Duseks.

The Charles Bridge is the oldest in Prague and dates back to 1357. Decorated with statues and sculptures from the 18th century, it crosses the Vltava River from the Old Town to a part of Prague known as Malá Strana or the 'Lesser Town'. In the main square is the St Nicholas Church, the most significant baroque structure in the city.

ABOVE: *Prague is built on the winding Vltava River which is celebrated in Smetana's evocative symphonic poem Má Vlast (My Country).*
FOLLOWING PAGES: *The beautifully preserved medieval town of Český Krumlov which is also situated on the Vltava River.*

Built between 1704 and 1755, the church's interior is dramatically decorated, and Mozart played the organs here during his visit of 1787. At that time St Nicholas had three organs, but one has since disappeared after it was transferred to another church.

Prague undoubtedly took Mozart to its heart. Shortly after his death the whole city paid tribute to him through a number of performances of his *Requiem*.

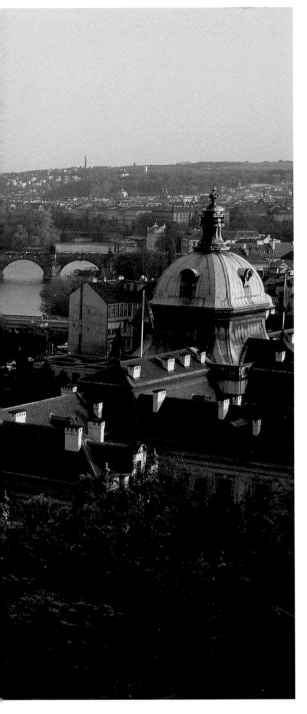

RIGHT: A detail of one of the two organs in the 'Lesser Town' St Nicholas church that were played by Mozart during his visit to Prague in 1787. At this time, there were actually three organs in the church, but one has since disappeared.

BELOW: So well preserved is the town of Český Krumlov that it is one of the UNESCO World Cultural Heritage sites. (BELOW) The Vltava River.

OPPOSITE: The Mansion Tower rises above the narrow, cobblestone streets — the castle dates back to mid-13th century.

No matter how popular Mozart might have been in Prague, the fact remains that it's best known as Dvořák's city, and one of the most charming buildings from the baroque period is now the Dvořák Museum. Established in 1932, it houses memorabilia, music scores, photographs, his piano, his desk and his viola. The building itself and the garden have been beautifully restored after having fallen into decay over a hundred years ago. Every year, the Museum conducts a remembrance ceremony at Dvořák's grave in Prague's Slavin Cemetery where Bedřích Smetana is also buried. Through their evocative music — notably Dvořák's *From The New World* and Smetana's *Má Vlast* — both composers eloquently conveyed the irrepressible spirit of Bohemia, reflected in both its culture and landscape. A spirit that's still very much in evidence today.

Long before it reaches Prague, high in the Bohemian Plateau, the Vltava River winds several times through the town of Český Krumlov. The town is one of the jewels in the crown of Europe — and most of the world doesn't even know it's here which is perhaps why it's been so beautifully preserved.

The castle overlooking the town dates back to around 1250, although most of the building took place between the 14th and 19th centuries.

Its size and the way it has been preserved, both architecturally and culturally is awe-inspiring. Among its many wonders is a rococo theatre complete with the original stage handling machinery. In 1992 the whole complex was added to the list of World Cultural Heritage sites.

Hotels

Classical Destinations would like to recommend the following hotels as stunning places to stay as you explore the destinations featured in this book and in the TV series. All these hotels have contributed to the making of the program and the publishing of this book, and we can speak from personal experience that you will be well looked after. You will find Websites listed for easy access and, when visiting these hotels in your travels, please do mention 'Classical Destinations' when you are booking.

HOTEL GOLDENER HIRSCH
Salzburg, Austria
www.starwood.com/goldenerhirsch
Located in the Old Town, a stroll to Mozart's birth house.

SHERATON SALZBURG HOTEL
Salzburg, Austria
www.sheraton.com/salzburg
A favourite during the Salzburg Festival season.

HOTEL AUERSPERG
Salzburg, Austria
www.auersperg.at
A delightful family alternative, close to the city.

HOTEL IMPERIAL
Vienna, Austria
www.starwood.com/imperial
Former Imperial Palace on the Ringstrasse.

HOTEL BRISTOL
Vienna, Austria
www.luxurycollection.com/bristol
Next to the Vienna Opera
House on the Ringstrasse.

HOTEL ALTSTADT
Vienna, Austria
www.altstadt.at
Stunning boutique apartment
residence.

SCANDIC EDDERKOPPEN,
SCANDIC BERGEN CITY,
SCANDIC ROVANIEMI
Oslo & Bergen, Norway,
Rovaniemi, Finland
www.scandic-hotels.com

FRETHEIM HOTEL
Flåm, Norway
www.fretheim-hotel.no
Norway's hidden treasure on
the edge of the fjord.

HOTEL ULLENSVANG
Hardanger, Norway
www.hotel-ullensvang.no
Stunning beauty, full of
Edvard Grieg history.

HILTON COPENHAGEN AIRPORT
Copenhagen, Denmark
www.hilton.com
Chic and contemporary, a
two minute walk from the
airport to check-in.

HOTEL KAMP
Helsinki, Finland
www.starwood.com/kamp
Sublime luxury, rich in
Sibelius history.

HILTON HELSINKI STRAND
Helsinki, Finland
www.hilton.com
One of Helsinki's top hotels.

HOTEL ASTORIA
St. Petersburg, Russia
www.astoria.spb.ru
Old world luxury, charm and
sophistication – stunning
location.

WESTIN PALACE
Milan, Italy
www.starwoodhotels.com/westin
Luxurious old world comfort
and service.

HOTEL METROPOLE
Venice, Italy
www.hotelmetropole.com
Perfect location, rich in
Vivaldi history.

HOTEL DANIELI
Venice, Italy
www.starwood.com/danieli
A former palace on the
waterfront near St. Mark's.

VILLA RINASCIMENTO
Lucca, Italy
www.villarinascimento.it
A rustic Tuscan hide-away.

LA PRINCIPESSA
Lucca, Italy
www.hotelprincipessa.com
A classical country residence
at the base of the hills
surrounding Lucca.

LOCANDA DEL LUPO
Parma, Italy
www.locandadellupo.com
A carefully restored historic
hotel preserving a distinctive
atmosphere with great dining.

ROYAL VICTORIA HOTEL
Pisa, Italy
www.royalvictoria.it
For those who are sensitive
to culture, with a charming
outlook.

HOTEL FUERSTENHOF
Leipzig, Germany
www.starwood.com/leipzig
Sublime luxury, on the edge
of the city.

WESTIN, LEIPZIG
Leipzig, Germany
www.starwood.com/leipzig
A favourite during the Bach
Festival.

HOTEL ELEPHANT
Weimar, Germany
www.starwood.com/weimar
A short walk from the front
door to the Town Square.

THE WESTIN GRAND BERLIN
Berlin, Germany
www.westin.com/grandberlin
Luxury and sophistication in
the heart of Berlin.

HOTEL KONIGSHOF
Bonn, Germany
www.hotel-koenigshof-bonn.de
On the banks of the Rhine,
next to the city centre.

GRAND HOTEL PETERSBURG
Bonn, Germany
www.gaestehaus-petersberg.de/ns.htm
Classic elegance, stunning
views overlooking the Rhine.

THE COURTYARD BY MARRIOTT
Eisenach, Germany
http://marriott.com/property/property
page/EIBCY
Family hotel offering access
to the Wartburg Castle.

INTERCONTINENTAL HOTEL
Prague, Czech Republic
www.prague.intercontinental.com
Five star, overlooking the
river, near the Rudolfinum
concert hall.

Classical Destinations Educational

Get your students to engage with classical music

Classical Destinations has also produced *Classical Destinations — A Classroom Guide to Classical Music*, a cutting-edge multi-media educational series for the classroom, college and for the home, delivered on DVD.

A unique supplementary learning program for middle and junior high schools, Classical Destinations offers an innovative multimedia learning kit that provides young students with a new and engaging route into classical music. The core objective of the series is to get every student in the class participating in classical music, whether or not they have previous knowledge or experience.

The series

Videos, audio, interactive and printed materials combine in an ambitious resource that explores the soundworlds, styles and contexts of the Western classical music heritage. This is a truly innovative and unique supplementary music curriculum that requires students to use their visual and aural senses, and which develops their potential through practical, creative and research activities.

Aimed primarily at 9 to 16 year- olds, Classical Destinations will be used in middle and junior high schools. A wide range of musical activities and assignments can be approached through full-class, small groups or individual situations. Each kit provides at least 13 hours of learning activity.

There are six DVD/CD-ROM packages in the series (released individually or as a boxed set), each centered on a specific country, and featuring some of the great composers and their music.

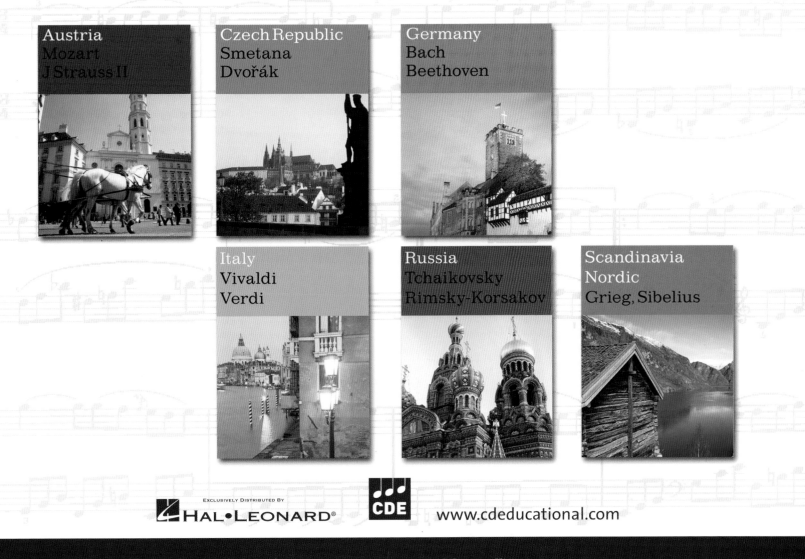

Austria
Mozart
J Strauss II

Czech Republic
Smetana
Dvořák

Germany
Bach
Beethoven

Italy
Vivaldi
Verdi

Russia
Tchaikovsky
Rimsky-Korsakov

Scandinavia
Nordic
Grieg, Sibelius

Austria (featuring Mozart & J Strauss II)
Czech Republic (featuring Smetana & Dvořák)
Germany (featuring Bach & Beethoven)
Italy (featuring Vivaldi & Verdi)
Russia (featuring Tchaikovsky & Rimsky-Korsakov)
Scandinavia/Nordic (featuring Grieg & Sibelius)

Please visit your local music store or call 800-637-2852. To order online visit musicdispatch.com

Companion CD and DVD

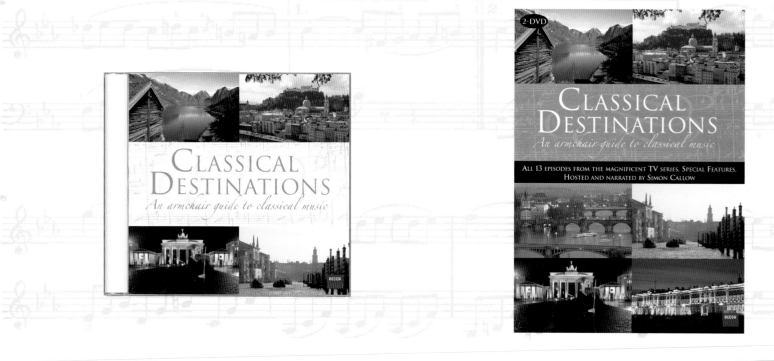

Experience the magic of *Classical Destinations* at your leisure with the *Classical Destinations* DVD — released on Decca, one of the world's leading classical record labels. This superbly presented double-DVD set includes special features not seen on TV, as well as all 13 episodes of the magnificent TV series.

The *Classical Destinations* DVD makes the perfect gift to people of all ages — or just treat yourself!

The double-CD set features highlights from the rich and diverse music that so prominently features throughout the TV series. It includes the TV theme performed by Niki Vasilakis. Take a unique journey through Europe's most beautiful cities, all to the immortal music of the world's greatest classical composers.

Niki Vasilakis performs in St. Thomas's Church, Leipzig, where Johann Sebastian Bach spent the last 27 years of his life as Cantor.

Partners and Sponsors

The following partners are acknowledged for their support and assistance in the production of this book, the TV series and companion products.

Fuji Film — www.fujifilm.com.au

WriteLight Pty Ltd — www.writelight.com.au

Decca Music Group, Universal Music — www.decca.com

Austrian Airlines — www.aua.com

Finnair — www.finnair.com

Starwood Hotels and Resorts — www.starwoodhotels.com

Phoenix Offset, Hong Kong

Graphic Print Group, Adelaide

Scandic Hotels — www.scandic-hotels.com

TOURIST AUTHORITIES:

Austrian National Tourist Office — www.austria-tourism.at

Vienna Tourist Board — www.vienna.info

Tourismus Salzburg GmbH — www.salzburg.info

Linz City Tourist Board — www.linz.at

Schloss Esterházy Management — www.schloss-esterhazy.at

Italian Government Tourist Office — www.enit.it

AND TOURIST REGIONS OF:

Tuscany — www.turismo.toscana.it

Lucca — www.luccaturismo.it, www.comune.lucca.it

Parma — www.turismo.parma.it, www.comune.parma.it

Pisa — www.pisa.turismo.toscana.it, www.comune.pisa.it

Venice — www.turismovenezia.it, www.turismo.provincia.venezia.it, www.comune.venezia.it

Viareggio — www.comune.viareggio.it, www.versilia.turismo.toscana.it

German National Tourist Office — www.germany-tourism.de

Tourism & Congress Bonn, Germany — www.bonn-region.de

Berlin Tourism & Marketing — www.berlin-tourist-information.de

Leipzig Tourist Service — www.leipzig.de

Eisenach Tourism — www.eisenach-tourist.de

Czech Tourism — www.czechtourism.com

Finnish Tourist Board — www.visitfinland.com

Helsinki City Tourist & Convention Bureau — www.hel.fi

Bergen Tourist Board — www.visitbergen.com

Oslo Tourism — www.visitoslo.com

Fjord Tours — www.fjordtours.no

Flåm Tourism — www.visitflam.com

Copenhagen Tourism — www.visitcopenhagen.dk

LOCATIONS:

AUSTRIA

Schönbrunn Palace, Vienna

Strauss Museum, Vienna

Vienna State Opera House

St. Stephen's Cathedral, Vienna

House of Music, Vienna

Eroica House, Vienna

Hotel Fottinger — Steinbach, (Mahler Hut)

Schlossverwaltung Hellbrunn, Salzburg

Hohensalzburg Fortress, Salzburg

St. Peter's Cathedral, Salzburg

Mozart Geburthaus, Salzburg

Mozart Wohnhaus, Salzburg

Schloss Mirabell, Salzburg

Schloss Leopoldskron, Salzburg

NORWAY

Edvard Grieg Museum, Troldhaugen

Vigeland Sculpture Park, Oslo

Akershus Fortress & Castle, Oslo

National Gallery, Oslo

Village of Undredal

Otternes Farmyard, Flåm

FINLAND

Lutheran Cathedral, Helsinki

'Ainola' — Home of Sibelius, Järvenpää

LAPLAND

Santa's Head Office, Arctic Circle

Arctic Circle Reindeer Farm

Lapland Safaris

ST PETERSBURG

The Hermitage

Pavlovsk Palace

Peter & Paul Fortress & Cathedral

Yusupov Palace

Mariinsky Theatre

St. Isaac's Cathedral

Rimsky-Korsakov Museum

Sheremetyev Palace — Museum of Ancient Instruments

ITALY

St. Mark's Basilica, Venice

Church of La Pietà, Venice

Museo Villa Puccini, Torre Del Lago

Villa Verdi, Sant'Agata

GERMANY

Church of St. George, Eisenach

Opera Leipzig

Bach House, Eisenach

St. Thomas's Church, Leipzig

St. Nicholas Church, Eisenach

Mendelssohn House, Leipzig

Wagner Exhibition, Eisenach

Beethoven Haus/Concert Hall, Bonn

St. Remigius Church, Bonn

Museum of Contemporary History, Bonn

PRAGUE

St. Nicholas Cathedral

National Theatre

Estates Theatre

Dvořák Hall — Rudolfinum

St. Vitus Cathedral — Prague Castle

Villa Bertramka

SPECIAL THANKS TO:

Vienna Boys Choir

Puccini Festival

Published in 2006 by Amadeus Press
512 Newark Pompton Turnpike
Pompton Plains, New Jersey 07444
www.amadeuspress.com

Created by Classical Destinations Pty Ltd
9 Ocean Street, North Avoca, NSW 2260, Australia
www.classicaldestinations.com

Text by Matt Wills & Paul Burrows adapted from the *Classical Destinations* television series
scripts written by Matt Wills © Classical Destinations Pty Ltd
Photography Wendy McDougall © Classical Destinations Pty Ltd

Concept/Executive Producer: Peter Beveridge
Designer: Kerry Klinner
Editor: Paul Burrows
Production: Victoria Jefferys, WriteLight Pty Ltd

First published in Australia in 2006 by Viking, an imprint of the Penguin Group

Prepress: Graphic Print Group, Adelaide
Printed in China by Phoenix Offset

Library of Congress Cataloging-in-Publication Data is available upon request.

Amadeus ISBN: 1-57467-158-8

ABOVE: The Grand Canal, Venice.
PAGE 1: The church of Santa Maria della Salute, Venice.
PAGES 2–3: Inside the National Opera House, Helsinki.